JOHNNY DEPP
The Biography

Nigel Goodall

BLAKE

First published in Great Britain in paperback by
Blake Publishing Ltd
3 Bramber Court
2 Bramber Road
London W14 9PB

A CIP catalogue for this book
is available from the British Library

ISBN 185782 3419

Typeset in Great Britain by BCP

Printed and bound in Great Britain by
Creative Print and Design (Wales), Ebbw Vale, Gwent

*The author wishes to clarify that Johnny Depp
was not interviewed for this book, and has in no way
co-operated with or participated in its preparation,
neither has he authorised it or its contents.*

Contents

Also Available by Nigel Goodall
from Blake Publishing

Winona Ryder: The Biography

About the author

Nigel Goodall is a British-born author with several bestselling books to his credit including *Cher In Her Own Words; Elton John: A Visual Documentary;* and *Jump Up: The Rise of the Rolling Stones.*

His affectionate biography of Winona Ryder, instantly acclaimed as the definitive account of the American actress, was nominated for the 1999 Samuel Johnson Prize for Non-Fiction, and chosen as one of the *Daily Telegraph* Books for Christmas.

He is also the co-author of *The Ultimate Queen* and several acclaimed books on Cliff Richard, and a contributing writer for *Johnny Depp: Movie Top Ten.*

He has also written a number of articles for numerous magazines, contributed to various album and video projects, and has recently joined Kfm independent radio as a showbusiness contributor. He is also an actor for drama groups in Sussex, where he lives, and claims to weigh the same as Winona Ryder.

Author's Note

I would like to suggest that this work is my story of Johnny Depp. For me, it cannot be *the* story of Johnny Depp simply because there is no such thing. Any biography, or even autobiography, can only represent an editing of the facts, a selection of detail and an attempt to make sense of the various, changeable developments of someone's real life.

It should also be noted that much of what becomes a story, whether formally or merely in relation to a dinner table anecdote, is based upon an interpretation of the facts. And facts can change, and new interpretations can at any moment alter our perspective of them.

If I have succeeded in my aim, I have given the reader the tools to create his or her own portrait of Johnny Depp, one of Hollywood's most respected young actors — and a true American original.

Nigel Goodall

To Peter Lewry,
my closest friend and colleague for 21 years.
Thank you for everything.

Acknowledgements

In November 1998, I asked Johnny Depp via his publicist, Leslee Dart, whether he would be interested in co-operating with a biography to be published in the year of his 36th birthday. During a lengthy and impeccably polite telephone conversation with Leslee some weeks later, she made it clear that Johnny was uncomfortable with the idea. John Blake, my publisher, was so persuasive, however, that I decided to go ahead with the book, and I informed Leslee of my intentions. In February 1999, after several more conversations, I received a letter from Leslee instructing me that Johnny was still not interested in contributing to or participating in a biography of himself at this time.

Although it is always strange to write a biography without the co-operation of the subject, in this case it has been a fascinating and worthwhile exercise to study this unique actor and musician, and one which I hope Johnny himself will consider accurate and objective.

Of those who did help, I am especially grateful to my speedy researcher Keith Hayward for generously accessing so much useful material, and for enabling me to gain a greater perspective on my subject, and whom every writer should have as their researcher (but mercifully don't!); Charlotte Helyar for doing such a fabulous job with the illustrations; John Blake for publishing my Winona Ryder biography and now this; to Adam Parfitt for taking care of the nuts and bolts once more, and the rest of the Blake team: Rosie, Anne Marie, Ceri, Graeme and Jon for everything else; all the photographers and picture agencies whose work graces the picture sections of this book; Greg Hatfield at my American distributors, Seven Hills; and my children Adam and Kim who cared and shared.

Organisations and individuals who helped along the way were Scott Coldwell and Neil Milner, two of the world's biggest Winona Ryder fans, for making available an endless supply of cuttings, magazines and pictures on Johnny and Winona; as did Vicki McKay, the largest collector of Johnny Depp memorabilia who very kindly sent me hundreds of cuttings from her own private collection, and did her best to satisfy my endless demands for information from her superbly maintained Johnny Depp website; Peter Lewry for his unpublished article on Vanessa Paradis and all the support in the world; Joanne Linskey and Neil Lover for their constant moral support and sound counsel; and Gill Watson and Kathleen Kennard for the late-night stop-overs.

Among my friends and colleagues who provided support and encouragement were: Keith Bessey and Jane McKee, Cheryl Newman, Jonathan and Sue Terry (just married!), Julie and Peggy Pettitt, Ana Coldwell, Tim Spray and Karen Terry, Georgina Partridge at the Entertainment Group, Sandra Hayward, Adrian Rigelsford, Franki Watson, Katherine Andrews, Mat Smith, Eric Harshbarger, Laurie Bratone at the American Indian College Fund, Elizabeth Cunningham, Elliot Gould, Roy Galloway at Eastbourne's Curzon Cinema, Carole Lewry, Michael Wilson, Bob and Chris Costen, Caroline Osborn, Charlotte Tudor, Jayne Bignell, John Hughes at City Screen, Paul Kerr, Dominic King, and my would-be agent if I had one, Robert Smith.

I would also like to thank those who maintain the

following internet sites for their often unsung research efforts: *A Fan's Page for Johnny Depp*; *The Internet Movie Database*; the authorized Winona Ryder site (alas no more); *The Butthole Surfers Website*; *E! Online*; *Hollywood Online*; *21 Jump Street Web Site*; and *The Temple of Kate Moss*.

I would also like to thank the following magazines and newspapers for their coverage of Johnny over the years, all of which I consulted during my research: *Rolling Stone*; *Vogue*; *US*; *Now*; *GQ*; *Interview*; *Advocate*; *Vanity Fair*; *Icon*; *Harpers Bazaar*; *People*; *Hello!*; *The Face*; *The Guardian*; *The Observer*; *The Times*; *Heat*; *The Sunday Times*; *FHM*; *People Weekly*; *TV Guide*; *Studio*; *Movieline*; *Newsweek*; *Eva*; *Flicks*; *Daily Star*; *Sky*; *Chat*; *Chicago Sun-Times*; *The Mirror*; *Los Angeles Magazine*; *Total Film*; *Planet Winona*; *Daily Mail*; *Daily Star*; *The Sun*; *Cowboys and Indians*; *Shout*; *The Detroit News*; and *Winona Fanzine (UK)*. Thanks also to the journalists who have interviewed Johnny, and whose articles also formed a valuable part of my research.

I am also indebted to several books: *Burton on Burton*, ed. Mark Salisbury (Faber & Faber, 1995); *Chronicle of the Cinema* (Dorling Kindersley, 1995); *The Virgin Encyclopedia of the Movies* (Virgin Books, 1995); *Johnny Depp: A Modern Rebel*, Brian J Cobb (Plexus, 1996); *Winona Ryder*, Dave Thompson (Taylor Publishing Company USA, 1997); and *Hollywood: The New Generation*, James Cameron-Wilson (B T Batsford, 1997).

Finally, I would like to thank Winona Ryder whose long and very public relationship with Johnny Depp, and my own biography of her last year, inspired me to write this book in the first place. Just as in the movies, it seemed like the perfect sequel.

INTRODUCTION

'Biography' meant a book about someone's life.
Only, for me, it was to become a kind of pursuit,
a tracking of the physical trail of someone's path
through the past, a following of footsteps.
You would never catch them; no, you would never
quite catch them. But maybe, if you were lucky,
you might write about the pursuit of that fleeting figure
in such a way as to bring it alive into the present.

Richard Holmes,
Footsteps: Adventures of a Romantic Biographer

I first wrote about Johnny Depp in 1997. I did so because I was writing a biography of Winona Ryder, his highest-profile girlfriend before Kate Moss, and to whom his three-year engagement was an essential element of my writing about Winona. But I was not writing about his movies, image or popularity in the singular sense. I was writing about him because of his long and very public relationship with Winona, which seemed to me to cement their reputations as important cultural icons, more so than any other celebrity couple, even royalty to a degree. But I had no idea at the time how intriguing it would be to write a full-scale biography of the other half, and to complete my telling of one of Hollywood's most intriguing fairytale romances.

Intriguing because if you toss a rock in Hollywood the odds are reasonably high you'll hit some pretty boy haunted by his teen idol status and moaning about getting his due respect as a serious actor — precisely the kind of teen pin-up star Johnny Depp used to be. Over the following years, of course, since he has fronted every teen magazine at every check-out stand and every newspaper stall, the *21 Jump Street* star has made a concerted effort to leave his teen idol years behind him to attain artistic credibility in its stead.

He passed on the *Speed* role that catapulted Keanu Reeves to stardom; declined offers to play *Interview with the Vampire*'s Lestat, and Bram Stoker's *Dracula*, plum parts snatched up by Tom Cruise and Gary Oldman; rejected the mythic *Legends of the Fall*, and the *Thelma and Louise* hustler assignments later taken by Brad Pitt; and chose to bequeath the roles of Robin Hood and Charlie Chaplin to Kevin Costner and Robert Downey Jnr.

Instead, Johnny cemented his reputation in Hollywood by brilliantly portraying such outré souls as the lonesome, freakish protagonist of *Edward Scissorhands*, and the independent, cross-dressing *Plan 9 from Outer Space* director Ed Wood. As Johnny himself explains, 'I'm not Blockbuster Boy. I never wanted to be.'

CHAPTER 1

'There's nothing worse than someone
who considers themself a serious actor,
because an actor is essentially a liar. I make a living.
I definitely wouldn't call myself a film star.
I'm much more "in the trenches" than glittery!'

Johnny Be Good

Outside the home of his publicist one cool Sunday evening, in February 1997, Johnny Depp is on his best behaviour. He looks like a kid who is dressed up to meet his girlfriend's parents. A dark blue sports coat, grey polo shirt, tan pin-striped trousers, and black lace-up shoes. His famously long, tousled hair has been shorn into a Fifties-style buzz cut, and he is all charm — the sort of charm that prompts him to address women as 'doll' and 'sweetheart', even as he lights up a cigarette and checks that his companion is not catching a chill in the cold winter night.

Although he smokes, he condemns the activity as fervently as any anti-smoker would. 'It's a wretched, wretched habit,' he curses. 'It controls a person. It's so bad.'

It is only then that one can imagine the effect those same comments would have on passing journalists. Could this possibly be the worst sin he has ever committed against his body? Why was he condemning such a vice? Was it because the pain and turmoil in his personal life was simply cascading out of him? No, it wasn't. He was doing it because it was a new role. And he had every good reason to be playing it.

In less than a week, his latest movie would be opening. As he read the first reviews, he must have felt incredibly relieved that the test audiences and mass-market reviewers had responded so favourably to the film. Writing in Britain's *Daily Star*, the paper's film critic offered one of the most concise summaries, which was shared by most other critics. Mike Newell's *Donnie Brasco* was 'the finest gangster film since *The Godfather*'.

It was the true story of FBI undercover agent Joe Pistone, aka Donnie Brasco, who, in the late Seventies, infiltrated the Mob in what was to become one of the most successful mole operations in the history of the American Government's crack-down against organised crime. Nonetheless, it was a mission that exacted a devastating personal price on the man who was drawn into an unexpected and revealing friendship with the criminal he was supposed to be destroying, and in the process almost destroyed himself.

The idea that Mike Newell would take on the American mobster myth with a dramatic examination of the emotional and moral core of the tough-guy loyalty that usually goes unquestioned, almost beggared belief. It was as if Quentin Tarantino had announced an adaptation of Danielle Steel. The shock was understandable too, for nowhere in

Newell's career to date — from *Four Weddings and a Funeral* to *Enchanted April* and *Into the West* — had he suggested he'd even be interested in filming a true story based on Brasco's undercover life in the Mafia. But he was.

Even more intriguing was producer Lou DiGiaimo's attraction to the project. He had known Pistone in high school and continued to socialise with him as an adult, but he never knew the truth about his friend's job until Pistone hit the headlines.

'I had no idea he was working for the FBI,' confessed DiGiaimo. 'We used to play basketball two or three times a week and then, one day, he just disappeared without a trace. About six or seven years later all the New York papers had a front-page story about this FBI agent who went undercover in the Mob, and they kept using the name Pistone. At first I thought it was a joke. I was thinking, can it really be Joe? A few days later he called me and we had dinner. I told him right then, I thought this story would make an incredible book and possibly a movie. He hadn't thought about that yet and he just said, "Well, we'll have to wait until the trials are over." That took four years.'

About the same time as it took to get the movie into production, producer Mark Johnson recalls, 'We were in the middle of *Rain Man* when Lou DiGiaimo brought us this fascinating book. It seemed very much worth developing into a screenplay.' Johnson's first choice of co-producer was his partner Gail Mutrux; he called him as soon as he had finished the book, who in turn called Paul Attanasio, best known for his screenplay of 1994's *Quiz Show*. And, of course, he jumped at the chance of scripting the movie.

Recruiting Mike Newell as the director was equally

instinctive. 'We all felt that very strongly,' said Johnson. 'Mike could understand what was most important about this story; the vibrant characters and the both funny and tragic situation they find themselves in. I also think there's something appropriate about having an Englishman direct this movie because sometimes an outsider can see and reveal things about an American way of life that a native would miss. When I first went with Mike to Brooklyn for location scouting, it was like going on a sociological expedition.'

Yet it could have turned out so differently, Newell explains. 'I spent some time in Brooklyn where these guys are still running the same kind of businesses they always have: gambling and loan sharking and so on. I would go out on the weekends, drink and eat with them and hang around in their social clubs. Obviously, there was a lot they wouldn't show me, but I saw as much as I could. It was like being let into the heart of the tribe. They were very generous to me and I became very fond of them, so I had to remind myself that they also did horrendous things, that these men that I was having such a good time with were also ... well, I didn't really want to know.'

Newell would work with that same sense of vigilance in mind as he set about selecting his cast. Although Johnny may have seemed an unconventional choice to many, he did prove to be the correct one. 'This particular role interested him, I think, because the whole character had to run beneath the surface, as it were,' Newell said later. And although the film buffs may be right when they say no one will ever displace Marlon Brando and Al Pacino as the godfathers of the mobsters, Johnny came as close as anyone. In fact, both

Godfather veterans called Johnny the best actor of his generation.

'He's very polite, a very gentle person in all sorts of ways,' Newell enthused. 'But I also think he has a devil in him. Underneath this wistfulness, you feel a sanction of violence. So there's this terrific mental energy going into keeping these two mutually antagonistic things in balance. That's what keeps you coming back.'

Asked why he chose Johnny, and not someone like Keanu Reeves, Newell was quick to reply. 'Well, I wanted someone who could act, for a start. And Johnny is one of those actors who acts in a kind of long term. You stay with his characterisations throughout a film because he tells you his story in his own good time, and more important, you are willing to wait for it.'

That is certainly true. All the same, Newell continues, 'Johnny doesn't suffer fools gladly. He tends towards a choice of material that's going to interest him intellectually, and has always said to himself that his career comes second.'

Denise Di Novi, producer of both *Edward Scissorhands* and *Ed Wood*, agreed. 'I was so thrilled to see *Donnie Brasco* because I think it was another level for Johnny. You know, a different character. I think he had really created a niche playing the strange guy, and the Donnie Brascos aren't your average person. I think it was a little broader context — the movie and the character.'

Johnny, however, was astonished when he heard what Brando and Pacino said. 'I don't know why people like that say those things, but I mean, obviously, that's great. I'm lucky to be able to say that they are friends of mine, but they are heroes, too. I have nothing but respect for them.'

Others on the *Donnie Brasco* set were well aware of what he meant. They also knew what it meant for Johnny to be filming in Florida, his own childhood stomping ground. As Jefferson Sage, the art director, would point out, it was the promised land, and an integral part of the filming. 'It's bright and colourful and a new start for the guys in the movie. Here was a whole new turf that was virtually wide open for them to exploit. It was exotic, warm and easy. But then that gets closed off to them and it makes coming back to Brooklyn twice as bad, you know, in the depth of winter and all that.'

The decision to cast Al Pacino in the role of the ageing hit-man Lefty Ruggiero was equally instinctive. As instinctive, in fact, as his acceptance. Besides, how could you go wrong with the actor who had established the archetype mobster as successfully as Bela Lugosi had the vampire.

Working with Al, Johnny continues, 'was everything and a whole lot more than I expected. It was a real treat and an honour. I learnt as much as I could, but it's difficult to pick out specifics. I expected him to be very serious and not very loose and playful, but he wasn't like that at all. He was constantly making jokes and making people laugh.'

The feeling was apparently mutual. 'Al was very, very relaxed and didn't feel that he had to compete in any way whatsoever,' Newell elaborated later. 'Johnny was working with Al very close to the beginning of our shooting and they were in a car. Suddenly, and absolutely unmistakably, there's this huge ripping fart, and Johnny said, "I'm terribly sorry, terribly sorry." A little silence fell, then there was another huge fart. Johnny said, "What can I say, I'm terribly sorry." And Al opened the window. Then there was a third one at which Al kind of looked at him, and then it was a whoopee cushion. And Al thought that was the greatest thing since sliced bread.'

In fact, it was the film's central relationship between Pistone and Ruggiero that most probably attracted Newell to the project in the first place. Certainly, the director focused on this element more than any other. How the undercover FBI agent adopted the identity of Donnie Brasco posing as a small-time Florida jewel thief, and Ruggiero, the lowly, embittered Mafia man who unwittingly vouches for him so that he gains access to the Mob world. It was a relationship that must ultimately be betrayed.

In the time Johnny spent with the former FBI agent months before filming got underway, 'I spoke about that with Joe. He said that there was no way you can hang around with someone for six years solid and not feel something for them. On the one hand, you can hate them and despise them, but on the other, you sort of love the guy.'

But, Johnny continues, 'it's wrong to say that Joe was betraying them. If he had been a Mafia guy from the beginning and then turned on his friends and associates, then that would have been a betrayal. But the fact is that Joe came in as an FBI agent and he was just doing his job. He made an enormous sacrifice. He missed his children growing up, he faced the daily threat to his life, and he had to move his family constantly to protect them. He is maybe the strongest person I ever met in my life.'

Pistone was also thoroughly enamoured with Johnny, particularly when 'all I knew about him was what I'd read in the papers. You know about him trashing hotel rooms and stuff. But we spent a lot of time together, we worked out in the gym, and I took him to the FBI academy in Virginia. He wanted to know everything.

'He would even ring my wife and ask questions. He kept saying, "I want to make this right for you because you have to live with this film for the rest of your life and I want to do it justice." And he did. Captured me to a tee. He absorbs so much, he doesn't try. It just comes to him. And he remembers everything. He's like a sponge. He wouldn't even go to see a screening until I could go with him. Most actors wouldn't care. They would just take the money and run. He's a lovely guy.'

Newell agrees with him. But he also explains it was the 'novel point of view about the Mob' that also attracted him, the idea that Brasco is 'a hard and brutal man' operating in a narrative that offers him no convenient escape clauses, no soft or fanciful evasions of fate. As much as anything else, Newell focused on creating an epic of heartbreak that defies even the most cynical viewer's urge to simply grab the title character by the throat and shout 'Fool!'

He is forced to abandon his real family for his Mob family. His wife's patience with his absences finally runs out and he must ultimately betray his only real friend in the criminal clan for the law enforcement bureaucrats who show not an ounce of understanding, let alone compassion for the soul Brasco has tortured in their service.

That ability is what lends *Donnie Brasco* its morally estranged edge, a blade that can slice friendship and trust in two. If nothing else, *Brasco* is a portrait of secretiveness, watchfulness, danger, duplicity and disguise.

Even with the movie's scope so sharply focused,

there were still times when Pistone was resistant to what was being filmed. One of those occasions, Newell remembers, was when 'we were shooting the scene where Johnny as Pistone hits his wife. Pistone was around on the set and there was a fantastic hoo-hah. It took the producer a whole morning to calm him down. He said he would never have hit his wife, and I believe him. But I insisted this was fiction.'

Another time was while the cast and crew were filming in New York, one of four locations commandeered for several scenes. This time, Newell complains, 'I had a woman come up to me in the street and spit in my face; "You think it's a joke! But it's not a joke. That bastard put my husband away. He stacked all the chips against him. He gave false testimony!" So I asked Pistone, did you? And he said, "Absolutely not, I proved all my cases."'

What must be remembered, however, is that the evidence collected by 'Donnie Brasco' led to over 200 indictments and over 100 convictions, and although Pistone continues to live with his wife under an assumed name in an undisclosed location, there is still a $500,000 open contract on his head.

Not that Pistone was convinced he was in any danger. According to Newell, 'He says he isn't because the guys who would carry it out are either in jail or they're too old. Or it's simply that Mob leadership changes. But what he does feel in danger from — and he travels around in disguise, armed all the time — is that some daft kid will come up to him in a bar and shoot him out of a clear blue sky, as a trophy scalp. Something the kid will get kudos from.'

There were, after all, the mobsters in Brooklyn. The same ones Johnny encountered while preparing for his role. 'I found the majority of them to be good guys — real, real gentlemen, family men, good fathers, good husbands. I had the utmost respect for the guys that I met — not exactly what we've come to know in the movies, that sort of wise-guy persona.'

All the same, Newell added, 'They're like unruly children. They'll do the most charming things and then they'll do the most savage things, sometimes almost in the same breath.'

Johnny elaborates. 'I don't think that they're serial killers. Let's put it this way. I think there's a circle in which they live, and within that circle there's a game of survival. But you can tag this to anyone who is, you know, living and has a pulse. That tag would be, if it's him or me, he's going down. I mean, I can't be any more plain than that. That's just the way it is. If somebody's gonna get ya, you're gonna try and get 'em first.'

As a child, it was something Johnny's mother Betty Sue advised him to do. 'She told me when I was really little that you get in a fight with somebody and they're bigger than you, you pick up the biggest fucking brick you can find, and you lay 'em out, you just fucking knock 'em out. I'll never forget it.' Although he may not have been old enough then to understand exactly what she meant, he does today. That's why,' he added, 'my mom is one of my best friends.'

The other self-defence tactic, of course, was guns. 'I have a few in the house, just in case some nightmare happens. I sometimes go shooting as well. Out into the desert and set up beer cans, because when they get really hot and you hit one, there's an enormous explosion. It's nice. I never shoot moving targets though. And living things are out.' His father, on the other hand, he explained, 'has been trying to get me to hunt with him for years. He hunts wild boar. But I can't kill an animal. I can eat quite a few, but I just can't shoot them.'

Although Pistone would most probably agree with that, he wasn't quite so happy with the suggestion that he betrayed the people he was infiltrating. In reality, he argued, 'it was my job'. Yet when he watched the movie for the first time, Newell added, 'He was in tears, really weeping. And I can only guess what was going on inside him. We presented the ethical and emotional side of this case as sharply as we could, and it got to him. If you live with these guys for seven or eight years and they wind up dying grisly deaths it would get to anybody, but Pistone was brilliant when he talked about living with them.'

Newsweek's Karen Schoemer said Johnny's performance was brilliant, especially, she added, as it was 'from someone who has admitted taking drugs as a teenager and who was arrested three years earlier for trashing a fancy New York hotel room'.

So isn't it surprising that Johnny and, not least, Al Pacino, were completely overlooked by the Golden Globe and Oscar committees even though the word around Hollywood predicted Pacino to be a clear favourite for an Oscar nomination. It just didn't seem feasible that the film could go completely unnoticed in the plethora of the two award shows.

Still, it wasn't the first time that Johnny's work had gone completely unappreciated. But he hadn't, *Newsweek* continued to acknowledge, 'become one of the best actors of his generation by playing nice, normal, aw-shucks guys next door. Peers like Brad Pitt and Keanu Reeves may have better track records at the box-office, but Depp has one up on them. He takes chances and he's created a body of work that actually makes sense when taken as a whole.

'The fractured fairytale boy in *Edward Scissorhands*; the beleaguered family caretaker in *What's Eating Gilbert Grape?*; even the morally estranged FBI agent in *Donnie Brasco* share a common bond — they're good-hearted people who find themselves unable to connect with the ones they love.' It was one of the things his characters did best.

Even as he sat down on his publicist's terrace, a few pale stars showed through the exposed winter frame of an overhead trellis. Aeroplanes flew low in the sky. Unexpected things started to happen. Even a bug fell into a glass of water just as his companion was about to drink it. 'Is he dead?' Johnny asked with genuine concern for the bug.

Not surprising, really, when you consider that Johnny loves bugs. He collects them, mounted traditionally with pins in glass boxes. At around seven years old, he explains, 'I used to catch chameleons and train them. I'd put them on my finger, and if they tried to move I'd flick 'em! I was sure I was going to be Lizard-Snake Expert guy.'

Spiders, however, were not a favourite. And Johnny makes no bones about the impact they had on his life. 'I'm really scared of them,' he confessed. Not even when a friend went out and bought him a tarantula for his birthday did it help. 'I thought, well, this is great. Now maybe I won't be scared of them any more. So I'd try to touch him and when I did, I'd scream. So I had to get rid of him.'

It wasn't as easy for him to rationalise his public profile either to himself or to others. 'It's really odd,' he observed, 'but people perceive me as some hotel-wrecking, drug-addled fiend. I'm not remotely close to that, not slightly.' It really didn't make any sense to him that those same people may have thought differently, even reacted differently, 'if I hadn't brought out my past'.

CHAPTER 2

'In my high school, there were different
classes of people: the jocks, the smart kids,
and the rednecks. Then there were
the burnouts. None of the girls wanted
to hang out with me. I was just,
you know, a kind of weedhead — a weird kid.'

Rebel With A Cause

John Depp and his wife Betty Sue were living in Owensboro, Kentucky, during the summer of 1963. The couple already had three children, two of them from Betty Sue's first marriage — two daughters, Debbie and Christie, and a son, Dan or 'DP' for short. Now Betty Sue was heavily pregnant with John's baby, their second together, and if everything went according to plan, John Christopher Depp II, Johnny Depp, would be born on 9 June 1963 in Owensboro, Kentucky. He was.

John Snr and Betty Sue could never have been described as anything other than typically conventional parents, and the world in which they circulated was equally typical. John was a public servant, working as a city engineer. Betty Sue worked as a waitress in a local coffee house. According to Johnny, years later, she 'cursed like a sailor, played cards and smoked cigarettes. And sometimes she would come home after working ten hours with $30 in tips. So in turn, when I was growing up, I just got in the habit of tipping.'

All the same, the Depps were, to all intents and purposes, a working-class American family, benefiting from the explosion of cheap tract housing first developed in the Fifties. They lived in a suburban town, had suburban lives and dreamed suburban dreams. It was, after all, the 1960s — the decade in which the post-war promises came of age, and the American dream was possible. If you worked nine to five, then why not? You could have the house, the car and the family, just like on the postcards and in the magazines. Heart and soul, John and Betty Sue were products of the Sixties.

But eight years after Johnny's birth, the war in Vietnam was still grinding on, and Nixon was still in the White House. And just three months after Johnny's eighth birthday, an American court martial finished trying the 25 officers and men charged with involvement in the 1968 civilian massacre at My Lai. Twenty-four of them were released unpunished. Three months later, the American airforce would commence its most intensive bombing campaign yet.

Insurrection at home was crushed no less ruthlessly. The horror of Kent State, where the National Guard fired upon unarmed student protesters, was still fresh in the mind when Attica State Prison in upstate New York erupted into open rebellion in September 1971. There, too, the solution was unbridled violence, as the prisoners' demands were answered by a thousand shock troops. And the first cogs in the machine that would eventually spit out the national humiliation of Watergate quietly began to turn. A dream, as the Depps had seen it, was ending.

Despite their convictions, Johnny wasn't about to be drawn into what he considered their suburban way of life. Neither did he want to emerge affected by the liberal principles to which he was now exposed, as his almost solitary life with his grandfather would prove.

As a child, Johnny would spend as much time as he could with him. 'I remember picking tobacco back in Kentucky,' he explained. 'We were inseparable, me and Pawpaw. He died when I was seven and that was a real big thing for me. But somehow I believe that he's around. I believe in ghosts. I hope I'm a ghost someday. I think I'd have more energy. But I'm sure my Pawpaw is around — guiding, watching. I have close calls sometimes. I think, Jesus Christ! How did I get out of that? I've just got a feeling that it's Pawpaw.'

Johnny's grandfather was a full-blooded Cherokee Indian who had the same haunting good looks, sharp cheekbones, and sculpted visage that Johnny himself would, in the coming years, lend to magazine covers the world over and cause much of American girlhood to fall for him.

The Depp family, although a fusion of German and Irish ancestry, were Cherokee by heritage. Even Johnny's version of his Cowboys and Indians playtime remained loyal to those same Indian nation bloodlines. Never once did he allow his Indian to be shot, wounded, die or even fall to the ground, no matter how many times his childhood friend, Sal

Jenco, aimed and fired off his cap gun pistol.

It was that fiercely independent spirit that was already firing the determination that would dictate his future. Johnny would simply not be assigned rules and regulations. He needed first to want it and feel it. It should come as no surprise that Johnny's first source of conflict with authority was his suspension from school for exposing his buttocks to a teacher. The command to carry out an everyday, mundane task was, in Johnny's eyes, simply the last straw.

But then again, 'I was a weird kid,' Johnny freely admits today. 'A kind of weed-head. I wanted to be Bruce Lee,' he remembers. 'I wanted to be on a SWAT team. And when I was five, I think, I wanted to be Daniel Boone.' But not everyone fitted into his personal iconography of heroes. John Wayne, for instance, was certainly a no-no. 'I know this sounds kind of anti-American, but I never could stand him. He seemed like such a right-wing, radical sort of guy.'

Maybe that was true. Maybe, too, his dislike of the celebrated screen cowboy had something to do with Johnny's own Cherokee heritage. After all, wasn't it Wayne who always made a habit of slaughtering hundreds of Indians in his movies? It is events like that which appal Johnny today. He still reels at the knowledge of how many distant relatives must have been lost in what he calls the genocidal murder of millions of American Indians.

In fact, it was the death of his grandfather, when Johnny was seven, that convinced the Depp family that the time was ripe to move, this time south to Miramar, just down the coast from Miami.

Even more importantly, moving to the working

coastal town was a step in the right direction for Johnny's father, who found work there as a public works official. And not unlike Johnny's own future of living in a succession of hotel rooms and rented apartments, his parents would check into one of the town motels, and would not move again for another twelve months.

In the end, though, Johnny recalls, 'We must have moved about 30 times. We'd go from neighbourhood to neighbourhood, sometimes from one house to the house next door. I don't know why. My mom would get ants somehow. But there's a huge history of my family out there. Furniture, my toys, schoolwork, everything, everything, everything was abandoned, left in attics or garages. All gone. We were gypsies, we lived all over the place, always transient. After a while, I thought, I'm not even going to introduce myself to the other kids.'

Those other kids, or schoolmates, Johnny found, shared very little common ground with him. But he didn't care. Why should he? After all, what on earth could a bunch of conforming school kids offer Johnny that rivalled the thrill of what he had in mind for his life in the small communal town?

It was, Johnny continues, like Endora, the dead-end town in the movie *What's Eating Gilbert Grape?* 'Where nothing much happens and nothing much ever will.' Not surprising really when you consider there wasn't much there other than the two grocery stores directly across the street from each other.

'There's a Winn-Dixie here, with a drugstore next door and, next to that, a card and gift store. Across the street was Publix, with its drugstore and card and gift store. The same thing, only different names. Either way, you were just there.'

And there was where he didn't want to be. It was probably what further complicated Johnny's childhood — the difficulty he encountered fitting in at school, for instance. 'I was not the most popular kid,' he mutters. 'I always felt like a total freak. That feeling of wanting to be accepted but not knowing how to be accepted as you are — honestly.' He talked on another occasion of 'wanting to hold a girl, but thinking I'll screw it up'.

In the years to come, of course, he would exact perfect revenge upon them all, by winning the affections of precisely the same sort of people in the movie *Edward Scissorhands*.

Right now, though, all he could do was hope it wouldn't be for ever. By his own admission and by his own lack of interest in his schooling, he arranged to sign up with the town's football team mainly because he thought it would please his father. But that didn't work out either. After a month he quit, and then wondered why he joined up and quit twice more.

But he also learned very quickly to pick up on other interests. Throughout his childhood, he documents, music was a constant passion, and one of his first real love affairs was with the band Kiss, whose performances were as outrageous as their music. He had even tried to emulate their vocalist Gene Simmons. He, too, would eat fire. But the day Johnny tried it for himself, his face went up in flames.

'I was, maybe, 12,' Johnny recalls, 'and we put a T-shirt on the end of a broom handle, soaked it in gasoline and lit it. Then I put gasoline in my mouth and breathed fire like

Simmons. Only it set my face on fire; I was running down the street with my face alight. Unfortunately, my mom obviously was going to see that my face was all burned up, so I lied completely. I said we were shooting fireworks off and one went off in my face. And she fell for it. She certainly didn't expect me to say, "Well, I put gasoline in my mouth and blew it into a huge stick of fire, Mom." The fireworks story was easier for her and me; and she bought it, bless her heart. It was one of the dumbest things I've ever done — not the dumbest, but right up there — and I have done lots of stupid things.'

In addition to his musical tastes, Johnny continued to share in the world's admiration of stunt motorcyclist, Evel Knievel, who in the late Seventies was wowing audiences with his death-defying leaps over rows and rows of double-height vehicles on his specially designed star-spangled Chopper bike. But as Johnny watched and played on, he also immersed himself in Vincent Van Gogh, as much for the artist's life and struggle as for his works of art.

Another obsession was the Second World War. As time passed, however, it must have seemed strange to his parents that he couldn't stop reading about Nazi Germany. Nor could he get enough of recreating imaginary episodes of *Hogan's Heroes*. In the back yard, he would dig a tunnel, clamber underground, and sit there waiting for the whole thing to collapse around him. It must have seemed even stranger when John and Betty Sue compared him to his friends. Even when he wasn't digging tunnels, he would be dreaming of becoming the first white member of the Harlem Globetrotters.

Equally influential in Johnny's upbringing, albeit for

different reasons, was his uncle. He was, Johnny explained 'a preacher who had this gospel group. He did the whole bit, where he stood up at the podium and held his arms out crying, and said, "Come on, run up, and be saved." And people would come up to his feet. It was that whole weird idol thing.'

Johnny, as much as anyone else in the congregation, couldn't believe how enthralling the art of performance was close up. He was even treated to a masterclass in capturing and holding the attention of an audience. And he witnessed the tricks and techniques his uncle used to convince his congregation of the truth of what he said, of the importance of what he revealed, and of the power of the artifice he employed.

His uncle often encouraged Johnny to express himself in the same way, whether musically or otherwise. Indeed, the influence of his uncle's approach to performance had already hit home. In fact, he couldn't wait to climb up on stage and try it out for himself. In such an environment, the idea of becoming a rock 'n' roll star became second nature to Johnny. Well, it sure beat the gas station attendant job that he feared would await him at the end of his schooling.

'My cousin had a gospel group and they came down and played gospel songs, and that was the first time I ever saw an electric guitar,' observed Johnny. It was how 'I got obsessed with the electric guitar, so my mom bought me one for $25. I was about 12 years old. Then I locked myself in a room for a year and taught myself how to play chords, picking things off records. That's how I got through puberty, just sitting in my room playing guitar, slobbering. Rarely do I remember seeing my family. And then I started playing in little garage bands. The first group I ever played in was called Flame.'

He even introduced a distinctive image for the band. 'At first we would wear T-shirts that said "Flame" on them. Next, at 13, I was wearing plain shirts. Then, I used to steal my mom's clothing. She had all these crushed velvet shirts with French-cut sleeves. And like seersucker bell bottoms; I dreamed of having platforms, but couldn't find any.'

Forever understanding, John and Betty Sue were still concerned about Johnny's schooling. It wasn't really going according to plan. 'I'd been in high school three years, and I may have just walked in yesterday. I had like eight credits, and I was in my third year of high school and I didn't want to be there. I was bored out of my mind, and I hated it.'

It was then, Johnny said, 'I hung around with bad crowds. We used to break and enter places. We'd break into the school and destroy a room or something. I used to steal things from stores.'

Even years later, when Johnny was asked for an autograph by one of his former teachers, he was outraged. 'I mean, what was I supposed to say? He'd failed me. I remember one time this teacher yelled at me so heavily in front of the entire class. He didn't have any time for me then, and now, all of a sudden, he wants my autograph? They all thought I was going to end up a drug addict, and in jail.'

And maybe they were right, Johnny concedes. It really didn't make any sense for them to keep him in the classroom when he wasn't exactly an exemplary pupil. 'I started smoking at 12, lost my virginity at 13 and did every kind of drug there was by 14. Pretty much any drug you can name, I've done it. I wouldn't say I was bad or malicious, I was just curious,' he admits. 'I certainly had my little experiences with drugs. Eventually, you see where that's headed and you get out.'

That proved to be the least of Johnny's difficulties. In 1978, when Johnny was 15, John and Betty Sue got divorced. It was the second time Betty Sue had suffered a failed marriage and things seemed to deteriorate very quickly from then on. Untreated, and certainly unrested from the emotional turmoil, Betty Sue was a broken-heart victim just waiting to happen. But the whole family, Johnny recalls, pulled together and did the best they could.

'Family is the most important thing in the world,' he says. 'Without that, you have nothing. It's the tightest bond you'll ever have. When you're in your teens, family's family. You think it's always gonna be there. You think, "I want friends and I want cars and I wanna do things different." But there's a certain age you hit when you realise, "What am I doing? This is my family." When my parents split up was when I think I realised these are the most important people in my life and, you know, I'd die for these people. I was 16, and it just sort of happened. You just deal with it, but there's no escaping the hurt. I mean, it definitely hurts.'

Johnny continues, 'I can remember my parents fighting and us kids wondering who was going to go with whom if they got divorced. When they did,' he continues, 'my father left and my mother was deeply hurt and sick physically and emotionally.'

Johnny elected to go with his mother, sister Christie, who is now firmly installed as his manager and adviser, and brother Dan, also now installed as the other half of his production company. Johnny's other sister Debbie went with her father to Hallendale where he still lives and works.

As for Betty Sue, Johnny, taking one step at a time, turned his attention to finding her a place of her own. He began looking around and found one north of Los Angeles. It is where she still lives today with her third husband, Robert Palmer. 'I don't sleep or eat much as a rule,' Johnny proclaimed. 'But at her house, I'm so relaxed, I immediately become starving. Then fall into this deep sleep.

'She's the greatest lady in the world,' he continues. 'Best friend, coolest thing. Just unbelievable. Her whole life she's been a waitress, but I won't let her wait tables any more.' And nowhere is that tribute better expressed than the day he headed for a local tattoo parlour and asked to have her name imprinted into his flesh inside a bright red heart.

He even made a note of when he had it done so he could tell his grandchildren. 'When I'm 90, and I'm sitting around and they go, "Gramps, when did you get that?" I want to be able to say 31 May 1988.'

And the Betty Sue tattoo would be discussed in much the same way as the Indian Chief's head he had engraved some years earlier, this time on his right side, in commemoration of his Cherokee heritage. If Johnny hadn't exactly told anyone about his intense curiosity in tattoos and self-scarring, he certainly sensed that people would soon ask. 'I remember carving my initials on my arm,' he once said. 'And I've scarred myself from time to time since then. In a way your body is a journal and the scars are sort of entries in it.'

He even developed elaborate plans with his friend

Sal Jenco to retreat from the turmoil of it all. The two were already seasoned veterans of everything imaginable. Now the two of them planned to live in the back of an old 1967 Impala, simply because Jenco had nowhere else to call home. It had, Johnny recalls, back seats filled with beer cans but little else. A far cry from the civilising essentials such as electricity, running water and all those other modern luxuries Johnny would now live without.

But in contrast to many of the journalists who have examined his early life in Miramar, Johnny balks at calling his upbringing wild and reckless. It was only after he became famous, he asserts, that he was tagged with those labels. Besides, 'the only reason that any of my past came out is because I brought it out. And the reason is that, hopefully, people can learn from it. Kids can say "Jesus, he went through the same thing I'm going through now. Maybe I'm not a bad kid, like everyone says."'

Everyone, he says, has conveniently labelled him 'a bad boy, or a delinquent or a rebel or one of those horrible things. To me, it was much more curiosity. It wasn't like I was some malicious kid who wanted to kick some old lady in the shin and run, you know. I just wanted to find what was out there.'

Nevertheless, he says, he had a fairly normal childhood. 'When you're 13, 14, and you hang out with a bunch of guys and the junior high prom just doesn't do it for you, you go out and do something. Experiment. You live in Miami as a kid, and drugs are everywhere. You try it for the usual reasons. Peer pressure, curiosity, boredom.'

CHAPTER 3

'I'd say I felt weird from the time I was 12
to the time I was 17, but then again,
during your teenage years, there's that feeling
of safety, like nothing can go wrong.
But that kind of feeling gets lost later.'

Rock Star No More

In 1979, when Johnny was 16, he still wasn't going to go back to school. He'd had enough with his fight for academic achievement. And he was tired of being the one who dreaded arriving at school every morning and finding that he had precious little in common with his schoolmates. When the rest of the class talked about *Star Wars*, Johnny would rave about whichever latest stunt Evel Knievel had pulled off, and when they laughed about last night's TV sitcom, Johnny would quote from *Hogan's Heroes*, the mouldy oldie that so enthralled him.

Johnny's musical tastes, too, were also unpopular at school. In the late Seventies punk rock was not exactly embraced by the musical mainstream. It was wild, weird, anti-social, and the people who liked it weren't much better. Indeed, when his schoolmates found out that Johnny liked the New Wave bands he was immediately regarded as an outcast. When they discovered that he was determined to pursue a career playing the same music, his ostracism was confirmed.

Johnny's band, The Kids, started out performing cover versions and warming up audiences for big name bands like the B52s and Talking Heads. And although they concentrated briefly on writing their own material (that Johnny would best describe as 'U2 mixed with the Sex Pistols'), they did little else.

'I'm sure my brain stopped at 17,' Johnny remembers. 'I was really happy then. I was playing in a band, reading books because I hadn't read in school, and there were girls around. In a way, I'm sort of stuck here.'

Forever persevering, the Kids next played some rock 'n' roll clubs in Florida. The only trouble, Johnny concedes, was that 'I was under age. But they would let me come in the back door to play, and then I'd have to leave right after the first set. That's how I made a living on about $25 a night.' There were, however, other times, when they ended up playing gigs for much more, sometimes for over $2,000. 'We used to make that for the entire group and road crew,' which, as Johnny would point out, was a huge sum at that time.

Around two years later, when Johnny was 18, 'we did two shows with Iggy Pop, and after, I got really, really drunk.' He was at the bar after the club had closed, getting ready, as Johnny puts it, 'to puke or something. And I saw Iggy in skimpy little pants wandering around the club with a dog. And for some reason, I started screaming and yelling at him, "Fuck you!" I don't know why, because I always idolised him. And he walked over, and just looked at me. I thought he was gonna hit me. And I said, "You little turd." And then he walked away.'

In the coming years, of course, the two would be reunited when they came together on the set of John Waters' *Cry Baby*. Discussing the incident then, Iggy Pop sighed philosophically. 'I was probably in the same condition as you, maybe worse,' Iggy said.

That was six years after Johnny had already become a musical hero himself around the usual Florida hangouts. It also proved to be the place where he met and eventually married Lori Ann Allison, a make-up artist five years older than Johnny, and whose favourite local band at that time was The Kids. She, too, had been trying her luck in music, as a recording engineer. But it was her sister Suzanne, now dating Bruce Witkin, another of The Kids, who apparently brought them together. If there were two people who could pull off a record deal for the band, it was Johnny and Lori. But their failure to do so, it was said in some quarters, contributed to the ending of their relationship two years later.

Others in the band were well aware of what they were going through, and Johnny remembers how he himself was feeling. 'I was married when I was 20. It was a strong bond with someone, but I can't necessarily say it was love. That's something that comes around once, maybe twice, if you're lucky. And I don't know if I experienced that, let's say, before I turned 30.'

It was also a sign of how quickly things could

change. 'I remember being in seventh grade and having the most intense crush on this very popular girl,' he admitted. 'I pined for this girl, like beyond *Romeo and Juliet*. Shocking. I just chewed my tongue up for her. Eighth grade comes along, we hang out a little at those parties where you end up making out. So we did that, and I just couldn't have been happier. Then she goes for the football guy, and leaves me just dangling in the breeze.'

Years later, Johnny continues, 'after I dropped out of high school, I'm playing a club. I'm on stage and I look out and I'm like "Fuck, it's her!" So I finished the set and I go directly to the bar where she's sitting and I walk up to her and it's that face, man — incredible. And I went, "It's so nice to see you!" And I look at her, and she's 250 pounds! She is mammoth, but her face is still the same. Again I went, "Oh my, nice to see you — how many kids do you have?" And she had four kids — what fitting payback for fucking breaking my heart when I was a little kid.'

All the same, Johnny simply put his time with Lori down to the process of growing up. Not even moving to Hollywood seemed to help.

'I guess I have very traditional kinds of sensibilities about that kind of stuff,' Johnny admitted later. 'You know, a man and a woman sharing their life together and having a baby, whatever. I think for a while I was trying to right the wrong of my parents because they split up when I was a kid, so I thought I could do it differently, make things work. I had the right intentions, but the wrong timing, and the wrong person. But I don't regret it. I had fun and I learned a lot from it.' More importantly, Johnny said, 'It wasn't working out, so we took care of it.'

Before the couple finally called it quits, Johnny, Lori and the rest of the band made what would best be described as an all-out last-ditch plea for rock 'n' roll stardom. 'Don Ray, a guy who booked all the bands at the Palace in Hollywood thought we should come out,' Johnny remembers. 'He wanted to manage us, so he pitched me some money and we saved up some money, and drove out there.'

But there was, of course, another set-back. The one that probably hadn't even crossed their minds. Getting the band working in Hollywood wasn't as easy as they had first thought. 'It was horrible,' Johnny admits. 'There were so many bands it was impossible to make any money. So we all got side jobs. We used to sell ads over the telephone — telemarketing. We got $100 a week for ripping people off. We'd tell them they'd been chosen by so-and-so in their area to receive a grandfather clock. They would order $500 worth of these fucking things and we would send them a cheap grandfather clock. It was horrible.'

Almost as horrible, Johnny confessed, as the little money he made selling personalised pens to companies over the phone. 'My first acting job,' he would smile later. 'I was working this day job selling ink pens over the phone and getting maybe $10 a week, and I thought, "What have I got to lose?" The last couple of times I did it, I just said, "Listen, you don't want this stuff, man."'

All the same, The Kids, Johnny says, 'did some good shows in LA. We played with the Bus Boys and Billy Idol.' But that's all there was more or less. Doing the same as they had done in Florida. If there was a career to be made out of playing in a band, hell, it sure didn't come their way.

Johnny and Lori took the disappointment stoically.

But still their failing hurt. They both decided to sit back and take stock of their lives. They needed to start putting things back in their rightful place. What they really wanted to do was sort out their increasingly ambivalent feelings for each other. As it turned out, one of those decisions was to dissolve their partnership in The Kids through divorce. They did that as well, almost two years to the day after they met. Johnny was 22, Lori 27.

Even worse, of course, was the pain that was part and parcel of the divorce. The same pain that Johnny and his parents had themselves lived through seven years earlier.

The only bright spot on the horizon was Lori's old friend Nicholas Cage. He was then the newly-emergent star of 1983's *Rumble Fish* and nephew of its director Francis Ford Coppola, best known at the time for his *Godfather* epics. He suggested that Johnny try acting. And with the help of his agent, he landed Johnny an audition call for a movie about to go into production with Wes Craven.

The director of such horror flicks as *The Last House on the Left* and *The Hills Have Eyes*, Craven's latest project was *A Nightmare on Elm Street*, a gruesomely bleak — and frequently unpleasant — slasher story. The screenplay, Craven's own labour of love, did not shy away from the explicit, to put it mildly.

Indeed, Craven had always been fascinated by dreams and the subconscious long before he learned he might be able to bring it to life on celluloid. During his first years of success, the fascination continued to gnaw at the director's mind. Then, some years before *A Nightmare on Elm Street* went into production, he came across a batch of newspaper reports about Laotian refugees so afflicted with horrifying nightmares that they became terrified of falling asleep.

It was this theme that he weaved into his movie, lending it a new character that would redefine horror as much as *The Exorcist* had done for the 1970s. *A Nightmare on Elm Street* defined slasher movies for the next decade and for most of the one that followed with such outings as *Scream, I Know What You Did Last Summer* and, of course, another four *Nightmare* sequels.

Not that Craven would have anything to do with them. When filming of *A Nightmare on Elm Street* commenced in July 1984 for release in October one year later, Craven had no intention of making any others. 'Why do a sequel?' he asked, when this one would be adequate enough on its own. Hell, how many times could the story be told before it would outrun its course?

Producer Robert Shaye, however, had different ideas. He and production company New Line Cinema had seen the potential for making further instalments and even asked Craven to shoot another ending for the continuity aspect of the saga. He refused, and remained in conflict with them over the next ten years throughout the following sequels, right up to his own, *Wes Craven's New Nightmare* in 1994.

It was the story of an outrageous new bogey-man, the hamburger-faced, razor-taloned Freddy Krueger, a child murderer who was burned to death after escaping conviction and who has now returned to his old stomping ground on Elm Street to haunt the inhabitants — mostly teenagers. There, they share common nightmares as Freddy, played by Robert Englund of television's *V*, stalks them in their dreams, using his claws to carve his way into their homes and their minds. Like some ghastly combination of Peter Pan and the Pied Piper, Freddy makes sure they never grow up.

Well, not exactly everyone. There was one who would survive the film's climax. Nancy Thompson, played by Helen Langenkamp, was the heroine of the piece. But it was the part of her boyfriend, Glen Lantz, who is violently sucked into a bed and churned out in a surge of blood and gore that Craven was now trying to fill.

Johnny, however, had second thoughts about pursuing the role. Even as he arrived to attend the reading he wasn't convinced. After all, he wasn't even remotely like the character he would be playing.

'I was just totally not what Wes had written for the story,' Johnny explained later. 'He had written the part of a big, blond, beach jock, football player guy. And I was sort of emaciated, with old hairspray and spiky hair, earrings, a little fucking catacomb dweller.'

The director had already sat through several other readings with aspiring young actors, but as soon as Johnny walked in, he knew his search had ended. There and then, he says, 'Johnny had a quiet charisma that none of the other actors had. He really had that sort of James Dean attraction. Just had a very powerful, yet very subtle personality.' Even Craven's daughter and her friends raved over him. 'They absolutely flipped,' Craven said at the time. 'He just had real sex appeal for women.' And he was perfect. Five hours later, Johnny's agent called to offer him the part. Now he was an actor.

And now he was about to taste the financial

rewards that his new career in cinema could offer. 'It was amazing to me that someone wanted to pay me that much money. Never had I seen anything like that.' Neither had he imagined the sudden thrust towards movie stardom, even though he really enjoyed playing the part of Glen Lantz, the dispensable kid who, as Johnny points out, 'got sucked into a bed. What kind of reviews can you get opposite Freddy Krueger for that? Johnny Depp was good as the boy who died?'

Indeed, he did. *Newhouse Newspapers* raved, '*A Nightmare on Elm Street* is the real thing. An outstanding example of a genre that would seem to have breathed its last breath.' *The Baltimore Sun* was equally effusive in its praise of the film: '*Nightmare* is so imaginative, so skilfully carried out and so effectively creepy that it has audiences and critics excited about the possibilities of the horror film once again.'

As the *New York Times* critic put it, '*Nightmare* puts the emphasis on bizarre special effects which aren't at all bad.' Britain's *Monthly Film Bulletin* agreed. '*Nightmare* is a superior example of an overworked genre, thanks to Craven's skill at organising individual shock scenes and getting neat performances out of his mostly young cast.'

Although Johnny himself would most probably judge that, in *A Nightmare on Elm Street*, he was some way from a career in movies, the film at least established him as a promising newcomer. 'I just kept working and I did a few more things here and there.'

One of those things was taking acting classes at Loft Studio, the Los Angeles-based drama school for what Johnny considered to be much-needed drama coaching. Not that his acting ability was likely to be drawn out of him in a conventional manner. And when he wasn't doing that, he filled his time with a few minor roles, including one in an episode of *Hotel*, and another in *Lady Blue*. He even played Sherilyn Fenn's boyfriend in *Dummies*, a ten-minute student film made for the American Film Institute. Otherwise, he found little else.

Well, not exactly little else. There was something — the lead role in another film called *Private Resort*, a movie about teen sexploitation. The ad slogan invited you to 'spend a riotous weekend at the hottest spot in Miami'. And another invited you to 'come to the wildest party of your life'. Either way, Johnny hated it. And so did the critics.

It was, according to the cover blurb on the home video, the story of two free-spirited teenagers, Ben (Rob Morrow) and Jack (Johnny) who check into the luxury hotel to pursue their favourite pastime — women! The object of Jack's lust is the rich, beautiful Dana, and he'll do anything — even pose as a surgeon — to manoeuvre her into operating position. Meanwhile, Ben's pursuit of a gorgeous waitress called Patti may be foiled by a house rule forbidding amorous activities bewteen guests. The boys' escapades are further threatened by a snoopy house detective called Reeves, and a manic thief nicknamed The Maestro, who are out to snatch a priceless diamond.

The climax — no better, Johnny complained, than the rest of the film — begins with the principal players running hell for leather after Jack and Ben. Even the occasional attempts to copy routines lifted unapologetically from countless Marx Brothers movies didn't help either. On reflection, it seemed there was very little on which to recommend *Private Resort*. Not even Johnny's nude scene 15 minutes into the film could soften the first reviews that rolled in following its release. Well aware of the movie's faults, Johnny most probably consoled himself in the belief that no one would ever see it. He certainly wouldn't. 'It was a stupid film.'

Another was the adaptation of Arthur Lions' acclaimed novel *Castles Burning*, a thriller in the Hitchcock genre that was made for cable television.

It was just a matter of knowing that 'I made some shitty movies when I was first starting out,' Johnny concedes. 'But I wasn't embarrassed by them, especially as I didn't think I was going to be an actor. I was just trying to make some money. I was still a musician. When I first started out I was just given the opportunity, and there was no other way to make that kind of money, apart from crime. I couldn't believe how much they were paying me.'

With his hair cut unfashionably spiky, only marginally distinguishable from his roles in *A Nightmare on Elm Street* and *Private Resort*, Johnny's character was neither well-defined or particularly challenging.

Donnie (Johnny) is the smart-arse son of millionaire Simon Fleischer, played by Dan Hedaya (who interestingly enough would eventually reunite with Johnny for *Benny and Joon* seven years later). Jacob Asch (played by Eric Roberts) was the gadget-ridden private eye, formerly a journalist who is hired by artist Gerald McMurty (Raymond J Barry) to track down his ex-wife (Beverly D'Angelo) now married to Fleischer, Donnie's father.

Asch's investigations, of course, uncover the usual cobweb of deceit that is part and parcel of such television movies, as well as Donnie's kidnapping and eventual, gruesome dismemberment. The geometrical convolutions are completed and, of course, further complicated by Donnie's conspiring girlfriend Emily (played by Pam Draper, Johnny's old ally from *Private Resort*).

And that was *Slow Burn*, a TV movie that, as one critic put it, was a limited exercise in recreating a lost genre of film. Johnny's rebuttal would have probably been equally critical. It would also have been understandable.

CHAPTER 4

'I know it sounds strange,
but I've never had much ambition.
I never really wanted to be an actor
or a director. I was a musician and still am.
The other stuff just happened.'

After the success of *Edward Scissorhands*, Johnny welcomed the opportunity to work with Tim Burton again on *Ed Wood*, an eponymous biopic of the occasional transvestite and worst B-movie director of all time.

Johnny's boyish charm in *21 Jump Street* made him an overnight pin-up.

Inset: Glenn in *Nightmare on Elm Street* was Johnny's movie debut, when he was literally swallowed up by a bed, in this, the first of Wes Craven's slasher movies.

Top: For *Cry Baby*, Johnny collaborated with famed director John Waters, for a role satirising his own teen idol image that drew comparisons to fifties rebels Marlon Brando, James Dean and Elvis Presley.

Bottom: Rather than accept the role of Charlie Chaplin in Richard Attenborough's movie, Johnny chose to play Buster Keaton in *Benny and Joon* with a disarmingly comic performance that earned him his second Golden Globe nomination for Best Comedy Actor.

As if to prove his diversity as an actor, Johnny followed *Ed Wood* with *Don Juan de Marco*. The choice also offered him the opportunity of working alongside Marlon Brando, one of his favourite actors.

Although it is not evident from his performance, much of Johnny's time shooting *What's Eating Gilbert Grape?* was plagued by emotional upheaval following his split from Winona Ryder. He is shown here with co-stars Leonardo di Caprio and Juliette Lewis.

Top: Despite a lukewarm reception to *Dead Man* at Cannes 1995, Johnny values the experience of working with co-star Robert Mitchum and director Jim Jarmusch.

Bottom: In October 1995, Johnny finally bought the $2.5 million Los Angeles mansion previously owned by *Dracula* star Bela Lugosi from the celebrity lawyer, Marvin Mitchelson.

According to director Tim Burton, starring in *Edward Scissorhands* together presented no problems for Johnny and Winona: 'They were very professional and didn't bring any weird stuff to the set.'

Al Pacino and Johnny received critical acclaim for their roles in the mobster film *Donnie Brasco*. Most credited it as the finest film of its genre since *The Godfather*.

A Soldier Boy And An Undercover Cop

With The Kids now disbanded and his well-received performance in *A Nightmare on Elm Street* behind him, Johnny, although still some way from being a great actor, hoped that *Private Resort* and *Slow Burn* might at least nudge him on his way. 'Well, I have no band,' he said at the time, 'and I've had some pretty good luck with this, so why don't I see what this acting stuff is about and just give it a shot?'

He did. The trouble was, he remembers, 'People weren't exactly banging my door down with scripts.' At that point he was about to give up on the idea of a career in movies, when out of the blue, the postman delivered a script accompanied by a letter suggesting he apply for the part of

Lerner, the hapless translator in Oliver Stone's upcoming *Platoon*.

Hollywood at the dawn of the 1980s recognised Stone as one of its most influential directors. Not only for his uncompromising approach to social and political issues, but also for his controversial treatment of them. Francis Ford Coppola and Martin Scorsese were probably his only other serious rivals at the time.

Stone first erupted on to the scene through his scriptural début, Alan Parker's unexpected hit, *Midnight Express*. That was eight years before he met Johnny, but since that time he had scripted another three films before turning his attention to directing after he was given the chance to take on the coruscating *Salvador*. The same year he would make his mark with *Platoon*, his startling Vietnam odyssey based on his own experiences of the no-hope war that the United States could not be deterred from waging despite widespread condemnation from the watching world.

Stone was similarly determined to get the movie made in the first place. Even though almost every studio and independent producer in America were less than enthusiastic about bankrolling the project, Stone simply defected across water to British producers and European funding to end up with a movie that would astound and overwhelm the year's Academy Awards ceremony at which *Platoon* was nominated in four categories: Best Picture, Best Director, Best Sound and Best Editing. It walked away with all of them.

Johnny remembers, 'I went to read for Oliver Stone and he scared the shit out of me! Then he said, "OK. I need

you for ten weeks in the jungle." It was a great experience,'
he says, even though at the time he was unaware of the
misery that was about to envelop him.

That misery, he recalls, was 13 days of hell. Not
only for Johnny, but also for the 30 other actors already
recruited from a newly-emergent cast that included Tom
Berenger, Willem Dafoe and Charlie Sheen.

In fact, none of them could believe the hard,
relentless field training they were about to be put through in
the run up to the six weeks principal photography on
location in the Philippines. Neither were they prepared for
the news that Stone had recruited a real-life Vietnam
veteran to knock them into shape.

The training programme, recalled by Dale Dye, was
intended to be difficult and physically demanding. 'I believe
that the only way a man can portray the rigours of jungle
combat is to get a taste of it.' That first taste, as Dye put it,
was the 60-mile cross-country trek from Manila into the
heart of the jungle that kicked off the first crucial round of
punishing routines.

Armed with baggy fatigues, jungle boots, dog tags,
rifles, bayonets, ponchos, flashlights, water canteens and
other infantry paraphernalia, the cast promptly set about
digging their two-man fox holes that they were required to
live in during the gruelling manoeuvres. Even worse were the
nights and days that ran into each other, the soaring
temperatures, the onslaught of red ants, and the rations of
'plastic' meat, cold hot dogs and tubs of what Johnny called
'bean something or other'. Not even the pre-cooked
hamburgers helped ease the torment.

No less demanding, of course, was the attention to

detail. Everything from instruction of M16 rifle handling to squad radio procedures, interspersed with Stone's own classes on scene study and character analysis. If war was hell, then this, Johnny said, was a close second. He hadn't expected filming to be so arduous. Nor had he expected to have much of his performance end up on the cutting-room floor.

Equally as tough were the 12, even 14-hour work days that Stone incorporated into the shooting schedule for it to be possible to wrap in 54 days. As Stone would later note, 'During the shoot, four or five production people were fired, and there were the usual fights, raging line-producer battles, several broken limbs, one near-fatal viper bite, hordes of insects, early monsoon rains, and too many scary moments in helicopters.'

Indeed, Stone went on to recall that the filming itself placed a lot of pressure on the cast and crew — everyone, in fact. Not insignificant was the unidentified fever bug that struck everybody just 12 days before shooting was meant to be completed. Most of them had suffered illnesses before, but they'd never experienced anything like this. An infection so debilitating that they had no choice but to succumb. That proved to be the primary concern out of all Stone's difficulties. All the same, he did eventually overcome it, even if it meant compromising on some of the shots he wanted to film, and he still made the schedule with hours to spare. Four or five, at least.

Not that anyone would have known. With an $8 million gross at less than 600 cinemas in its first weekend, Oliver Stone's *Platoon* enjoyed the biggest opening of the month during its February 1987 release. And the critics confirmed the public's approval by showering the film with plaudits.

Writing in the *New York Times*, critic Vincent Canby offered one of the most concise summaries in his praise for the cast. 'The members of the supporting cast are no less fine than the principal players, and no less effective, often, for being anonymous.' *Variety* agreed that 'each member of the young cast have their moments to shine'.

And New York's David Denby said much the same. 'Oliver Stone's impassioned, mournful *Platoon* is the kind of Vietnam film many of us have longed for ... easily the most powerful film of the year. There are many casting victories in this brilliantly acted film. You can feel the excitement of hungry actors seizing a moment.' Indeed, it was high praise. Not least for Johnny. In fact, he brought such a natural air to his performance that before the cinema-going public even got a chance to see him in the film, the critics were already on his side.

With his work on *Platoon*, and his divorce from Lori Ann Allison finalised just before filming got underway, Johnny looked forward to starting work on *Wonderland Avenue*, another Oliver Stone movie based on the autobiographical reminiscences of an adolescent throwaway who ran with Jim Morrison of *The Doors*. 'It's going to be an interesting, really dark movie,' Johnny said at the time. But only months later he had dropped out of the project saying 'it was taking too long to work out.'

Far more appealing was a friend's nothing-to-lose suggestion that he join up with Rock City Angels. He did. But two months after Johnny started filming *21 Jump Street*, the band, much to Johnny's amazement, signed with David Geffen's record label for what was reportedly the biggest deal since Madonna. Well, according to *Movieline*, it was, even though there was no second album. Johnny was less than ecstatic. 'All I wanted since I was twelve years old was to go on the road.'

Basking in the glow of playing with his new band, Johnny slipped almost unnoticed into his relationship with Sherilyn Fenn, his co-star from *Dummies*, and to whom, only months after meeting on the set of the student film, he was reportedly engaged, and was now living with.

Johnny Depp and Sherilyn Fenn — it could have been a relationship made in tabloid heaven but 'we weren't famous then', recalls Johnny. Fenn, best known at the time for her erotic performance in 1988's *Two Moon Junction*, was still some years away from her role as Audrey Horne in David Lynch's bizarre soap series *Twin Peaks*, and even further from replacing Kim Basinger when she dropped out of 1993's *Boxing Helena*.

Since *Slow Burn*, and far more importantly, *Platoon*, Johnny had been determined he would not return to the small screen, not even when he heard that Fox were trying to fill the part of Tom Hanson, an undercover high school cop for *Jump Street Chapel*, a new series pilot they were producing for network broadcasting. Neither did he want to read the script. It never even crossed his mind. The idea of a long-running television series just didn't figure in Johnny's professional priorities.

'It wasn't that I was snubbing television or anything,' he insisted, 'I just wasn't ready for that kind of commitment.' But that didn't stop the series creator Patrick Hasburgh wanting to cast Johnny Depp, the promising young newcomer from *Platoon*.

But Johnny, Hasburgh had heard through the

grapevine, wasn't at all interested. So the studio, already committed to filming the pilot, did exactly that, with Jeff Yagher of television's *V* in the Hanson role. But after three weeks of shooting, that idea fell through as well when Yagher was dropped from the production. The problem now was that Fox were so delighted with the shot footage that they promptly demanded more episodes, and even changed its original title to the newer, snappier, *21 Jump Street.* The only other stumbling block, of course, was they had nobody to play Hanson. Well, not exactly — there was still Johnny Depp.

'I got a call from my agents who said these people want you to come and read for this TV thing,' Johnny explained. 'But I said no, no, no. I didn't want to sign to some big contract that would bind me for years. So they hired somebody else to do it, and they fired him after a month, and then they called me again and said, would you please come in and do it? My agent said, the average span of a TV series is 13 episodes, if that. One season. So I said OK.'

Even though Johnny was now firmly committed to the idea of filming an entire television series, he still remained unconvinced about the project. His misgivings were principally due to the character he would be playing. 'Hanson is not someone I'd want to have pizza with,' Johnny noted unfavourably. 'I don't believe in having undercover cops in high school. It's spying. The only thing I have in common with Tom Hanson is that we look alike.'

Johnny's uncertainty was understandable. After all, he was a character who seemed to have more hang-ups than most. He was a 20-something second-generation cop who had the youthful appearance of a 15-year-old. The only difficulty is that his precinct colleagues and even the bad guys can't help rubbing him up the wrong way about it. And it's sinking him into a trough of depression, made worse by the fact that he needs to prove he's as great a cop as his father was.

Choosing between desk duty and joining an élite group of undercover cops is all it takes to recover his goals and ambitions. The group's mission, out of their abandoned chapel base, is to look young enough to infiltrate the local high school haunts to flush out the teens selling drugs instead of getting on with their studies.

Hanson, of course, has long wanted to join the squad that now floods the classrooms, which included Dustin Nguyen as H T Ioki, Holly Robinson as Judy Hoffs, Peter DeLuise as Doug Penhall, and, running the show, Frederic Forrest as Captain Richard Jenko, replaced seven episodes later by Stephen Williams.

Interestingly enough, the pilot was based on a controversial real-life operation which ran in Los Angeles in 1974. Indeed, the youth anti-drug programme made headline news the year before *21 Jump Street* aired on national television when one of the undercover agents allegedly developed a romantic relationship with a 17-year-old high school student.

For a time, Johnny moved his base to Vancouver close to the *21 Jump Street* set, and even moved his mother Betty Sue and her new husband Robert Palmer out there to join him. If that reunion wasn't enough to awaken Johnny's memory of his Florida childhood, then Sal Jenco, his friend from that time, certainly would.

He was visiting Johnny on the set when his party

piece of inhaling air and blowing it out like a strange-looking fish gave the *Jump Street* producers an idea. They recruited him to play a character nicknamed Blowfish, one of the regulars to drift in and out of the show during the series. Another friend, Peter DeLuise, was also given a small role, much to Johnny's relief. Both proved to be invaluable allies during and after filming. 'If Peter wasn't on the show I would have gone insane or jumped into the river,' Johnny says with a smile. 'He was my saviour.'

He also enjoyed his time in between takes on location with Sherilyn Fenn, and managed to secure her a small cameo role in the ninth episode. She would appear as the daughter of a police officer whose abusive treatment of her results in her contracting Hanson — now working undercover with Penhall as the drug-dealing McQuaid brothers — to murder him.

With prime-time viewing, *21 Jump Street* could do no wrong, and if it's true that every generation gets the show it deserves, there could be no better successor to *The Mod Squad* than this. Proof came in the form of the staggering 10,000 fan letters a month Johnny received; more than Michael J Fox, more than Charlie Sheen, and more than Rob Lowe, all of whom were newly-emergent stars in Hollywood at the time. But then again, affirmed Fan Handle, the Los Angeles star mail handling service, 'TV guys always get more than film guys.'

In the face of such success, Johnny would most probably agree. But at the same time, he couldn't help but be concerned. 'I've gotten weird letters, suicide letters, girls threatening to jump if I don't get in touch with them. So you think, this is bullshit, but then, what if it's not? Who wants to take that chance. I write them back, tell them to hang in there. If things are that bad they have to get better. But I'm not altogether stable myself, so who am I to give advice?

'Even kids,' he continues, 'write to me and say they are having these problems, or they want to commit suicide or something. It's scary. I have to say, "Listen, I'm just an actor, not a professional psychologist. If you need help, you should go and get it."'

It probably didn't help that he also took up permanent residence on the cover of *Tiger Beat* and numerous other teen magazines. Everything, Johnny adds, from '*Sixteen*! *Teen Beat*! *Teen Dream*! *Teen Poop*! *Teen Piss*! *Teen Shit*!' Even more damaging, he recalls, was the fact that 'I was this product. Teen boy. Poster boy. All that stuff that I wasn't. But they made me that. It was horribly uncomfortable.'

Equally uncomfortable was the image that had caused much of American girlhood to fall for him. The iconography of adolescent fantasy. 'It's terrifying,' he admitted later. 'People come up to you and start crying. Everybody compares everyone to James Dean. If you're lucky they mention Brando or De Niro. They invite you to put on an instant image.'

One of those occasions was when the *21 Jump Street* City Tour reached Chicago in August 1988. With echoes of the fan hysteria that greeted The Beatles' first American tour in the Sixties, screaming teenagers, men and women, would fight their way to Johnny for autographs.

Neither did he go unnoticed in the plethora of popularity polls with which the teen magazines at the time abounded. Not for the first time in his career, *Rolling Stone* voted him 'Hot Face of 1988', and *US* magazine tagged him one of the 'Ten Sexiest Bachelors'.

As for the scripts, he would question those, too. 'Sometimes there are things that I personally and morally don't agree with.' In one episode, he remembers, 'My character had to set a cross alight. It was supposedly dealing with racism, but I don't think it worked. I found it pretty repulsive, and although in the end I did it, I didn't think the episode dealt with the issue correctly.'

Another episode awakened a different kind of horror. So much so that he wouldn't even agree to appear in it. It was the story of a high school student deliberately murdered after being wrongly suspected of being an informer. Needless to say, the genuine informer stands by without uttering a word.

Johnny, however, spoke out. He pulled out of the episode after a squabble over moral issues, and even if the studio had begged him to reconsider, he was not about to 'sell out' his beliefs. 'I wanted no part of that one.' Fox simply told Hasburgh to write his character out of that episode's story and have new cast member Richard Greico's Dennis Booker take his place.

And in another story, Johnny again condemned the show's content when its theme centred around a student building an electric chair in shop class. 'I was very concerned from the beginning that *Jump Street* would never be preachy or point the finger. I'm not a good-guy role model. Hanson's pretty gung-ho about his job.'

Like others, Hasburgh could see that 'Johnny's a kid who has often experienced the same problems we're dealing with on the show.' Is it possible that Johnny could be put in the same category? And if he could, why on earth was he asked to film a public service announcement that said: 'Hi, I'm Johnny Depp, and listen; stay in school and graduate, because it means the world to me and you'? When Johnny heard that news, he couldn't believe it either. 'I'd been working for these people for four years. Don't they know I'm a drop out? How can I tell people to stay in school? Then they said, "Oh yes, we forgot."'

In the end, though, Johnny did agree to appear in some of the public service announcements that ran alongside the issue-based episodes. 'The first season we hit a lot of good ones,' Johnny explains. 'The second season, the same. We dealt with AIDS, sexual molestation, child molestation, things like that.' Unfortunately, 'Patrick left the show after the second season, and the direction seemed to change.'

Well aware of the show's faults from that time, Johnny also knew that *21 Jump Street*'s biggest downfall was the audience it was quite deliberately targeted at. But, he continued, 'I don't want to bite the hand that feeds me. The show has done a tremendous amount for me. It put me on the map. But in a lot of instances the people pushing the pens have been very irresponsible. And that's scary.'

The tabloid press, of course, was less cautious. Johnny's apparent on-set tantrums, misbehaviour and egotism quickly became newsworthy, and his alleged arrest for assault and mischief in conjunction with a 'noisy' party he attended in March 1989 simply added fuel to an already smouldering fire. Although Johnny feigned nonchalance at the time, 'I have a couple of ideas where the stories came from. I think that there are a couple of people who don't like the fact that I am outspoken about certain things. As far as temper tantrums and throwing punches at my producers, it's such bull that it's hilarious.' Far more important, he explained, 'I don't think my ideas or my principles have changed. But I've learned a lot about this business, how political it is, and how people manipulate other people. It's scary, man. Power is a scary thing.'

Certainly, that is true. At the same time, though, Johnny also recognised the advantage of taking over the directional seat for two public service announcements. One for a child abuse helpline service on American television, and another for the American Make a Wish Foundation.

'It helps cancer patients or people who aren't going to live a long time,' he explained. 'They write in and say, "It's my dream to meet Johnny Depp," or someone, and we meet up with them. It can be heartbreaking, but you meet a lot of very sweet people. I wouldn't trade that in for the world. Ego, money, career — you can take it all so seriously. But faced with a kid who's dying, it all means nothing.'

He even found time to appear in a 15-minute film short he made from a script he co-wrote 'about the things people can do to screw each other up'. And when he wasn't doing that, he would harbour his dream to star in a movie version of Jack Kerouac's *On The Road*, the same work Francis Ford Coppola, the *Godfather II* director, was interested in. A decade later, both Johnny and Coppola's passion for the project remained unabated. Not only that, but it would also feed Johnny's intense interest in Kerouac and the Beat poetry movement of the 1960s.

Nevertheless, he did have second thoughts. At one time, he even considered calling it a day. Going back to music was one option that appealed. 'I could do a Bruce Willis thing and do a record now, but it would just milk my teen boy, pop idol image. And I'd rather do nothing than do that. Music is still part of my life but I wouldn't want to do it now because of the way the people in charge are. They want to take you and make you into something you're not.'

Even as he turned 25 in June 1988, Johnny was rapidly tiring of playing the popular undercover high school cop, no matter how much popularity he generated. It was when he started another season for *21 Jump Street* that the weariness of it all finally exploded into the open. From now on, he announced that he would start revising the scripts. Lines like 'This is a great place, Doug,' would become 'Nice digs, Doug, you dog, dig 'em.' He also hoped it would lead to him being kicked off the show.

For another episode, he even suggested his character could be obsessed with peanut butter, and could get caught by the other characters smearing it over his naked body. In another tirade, Johnny complained, 'For the last two years I didn't even know what my character's name was.'

All the same, responded one producer, 'I don't always agree with him, but I can see where he's coming from. He fights hard for what he believes in and he has a tendency to fight for other people.'

Johnny, however, was adamant. 'My feeling is that the show needs to go deeper into certain issues, like racism and gang violence. In television there are strict boundaries, so there's only so much you can do, but the only way to change something is to fight it.'

Even when *Interview* magazine caught up with him

two years later, he told John Waters much the same. 'I think they should make the character start to lose his mind, because the hazards of being a policeman can make you go crazy. I think he should go completely insane. They should really break the boundaries that there are in television. They should put him in an asylum.'

Interestingly enough, a later episode did, in fact, have Hanson undercover in an asylum for juveniles to investigate alleged abuse by the staff on the residents. Hanson's feigned illness and drug addiction is so convincing to the staff that they lock him away, and refuse to believe his delusions about being an undercover cop.

Perhaps more episodes like that would have encouraged Johnny to have remained with the show longer than he did. 'I learned a lot of lessons from it,' Johnny would explain later. 'But when you're doing a series like that there's really no creative control. The word "creative" doesn't really exist in their vocabulary. So I said to myself that at the first chance I got, I was going to do exactly what I wanted to do and not compromise. And that's what I did. Since then, I've been lucky enough to do films I've wanted to do and to work with directors I've wanted to work with.'

Not only that, but Johnny felt no connection whatsoever to his character, Tom Hanson, not any more. He never did. But according to Hasburgh, Johnny 'was very, very new with enormous talents, and *21 Jump Street* was his garage band. And he really, really had an opportunity to hone his skills and his talents every single day. It was remarkable to watch this young actor get better and better by the minute.'

Denise Di Novi, who later produced two of Johnny's

movies, agreed. 'When you work with certain actors you start to have a respect for that magical thing that makes a film star. And people really do either have it or they don't have it. They don't acquire it. They don't learn how to do it. It's usually recognisable on the very first thing that they do. I mean you look at *21 Jump Street*. You know, find an old re-run of that, and see that, and you can say he had it on this stupid, you know, TV series.'

That was certainly true. Also true was the fact that, during this same period, Johnny and Sherilyn Fenn broke up. No explanation was offered, although insiders were quick to offer their own conclusions. Some even suggested that he was jilting Fenn on the grounds of her erotic performance in *Two Moon Junction*. This charge came despite the fact that most simply blamed the career conflicts that kept the couple separated for so much of the time. With all the attendant filming and personal appearance outings that *Jump Street* entailed, it wasn't really surprising. From that point alone, it seemed the relationship didn't really stand much of a chance.

Johnny, however, didn't remain alone for long. Some observers noted that he was now seeing Jennifer Grey, best known for her role opposite Patrick Swayze in 1987's *Dirty Dancing*. It was shortly after she met Johnny that he gave her an engagement ring, but six months after that, they had gone their separate ways. Once again, it seemed that most of the couple's life together was spent apart. Johnny was in Vancouver on the set of *21 Jump Street*, while Grey was away working in Los Angeles.

With Johnny's own spare time at a premium, as with Fenn, the relationship once again didn't really stand much of a chance, and although he reinforced that, he had very little else to say on the subject.

Besides, he didn't want that sort of hell. 'It's like when you're in high school,' he explained, 'and you're going steady with someone and your friends say, "Hey, man, are you seeing this girl?" and they start razzing you. If you love this girl, you're not going to tell your friends. I think you have to shield things; otherwise we'd all be out there cutting our arms open and showing you. Here's my blood. Have a vein.' Why do you think Elvis cloistered Priscilla at Graceland for what was Hollywood's best-kept secret?

CHAPTER 5

'People don't realise this, but we've been together
almost a year and a half. Out of any, whatever,
thing I've been through before, it hasn't been this long.
It wasn't like, "Hi, nice to meet you, here's a ring."
It was about five months before we got engaged.
They thought we ran away to Las Vegas and got married.'

True Love

The first time Johnny and Winona Ryder clapped eyes on each other they knew it was love at first sight. He knew he was looking at the girl of his dreams. Her stunning natural beauty just hit him. Everything about her was perfect. He didn't want to be seen staring at her as she got a Coke in the lobby of the Ziegfield Theater in New York but he simply couldn't help it. Not surprising, really. Squeezing herself into a tight white Giorgio di Sant'Angelo lycra mini-dress with plunging neckline, Winona was in town for the première of her film *Great Balls of Fire* in which she played the child bride of Jerry Lee Lewis.

She had already been wowing the paparrazzi with her arrival, and by the time her elfin frame moved inside,

Johnny couldn't help but notice the dark-brown velvet eyes that flickered adorably, or the gorgeous bobbed black hair that was swept away from her forehead to offset the pale porcelain skin that he thought echoed visages of a young Elizabeth Taylor with an equally enviable body. The message was simple. She was young, she was hip, and she was cool. Not only that but the whole world was in love with her, or at least those who had seen her movies were. From that point of view, Johnny was no different. The fact that she could also act the socks off her contemporaries must have helped.

Indeed, Winona had already proved that she could rise above the profit margin of the coins in the box office; she had ever since she débuted in David Seltzer's *Lucas*, the first of her many alienated teenager roles. A starring role followed in Daniel Petrie's *Square Dance* before she landed the part of the sensitive-souled misfit heroine of Tim Burton's *Beetlejuice*, and that of a teenage killer in Michael Lehmann's dark, satirical comedy *Heathers*. Both movies delighted audiences and critics with the appearance of a new fully-formed star as she all but took up permanent residence on the covers of the teen magazines.

'It was a classic glance,' raved Johnny, 'like that zoom lens in *West Side Story* when everything else gets foggy.' It wasn't, Winona said, 'a long moment, but it was suspended'.

Dressed more casually for when she was dragged to meet Johnny in his hotel room at the Château Marmont a couple of months later by Josh Richman, a mutual friend through the small parts he played in *Heathers* and *21 Jump Street*, Winona watched entranced by the charm that had caused much of American girlhood to fall for him, and was even more enamoured of the intelligence that his smart, sensitive *21 Jump Street* role had seemed to imbue him with.

Although at first, 'I thought maybe he would be a jerk. I didn't know,' Winona confessed, 'but he was really, really shy.' Shy or not, it was where Johnny and Winona began their intense and often unstable relationship. It was just six months before they were due to film Tim Burton's *Edward Scissorhands* together, although at the time, of course, they had no idea they would be working alongside each other.

Almost before they knew what was happening, they were arranging to see each other again. Their first date, a few weeks later, was a party at the Hollywood home of counterculture guru Timothy Leary, Winona's godfather. Johnny was simply ecstatic. 'When I met Winona and we fell in love, it was absolutely like nothing before. We hung out the whole day ... and night, and we've been hanging out ever since. I love her more than anything in the whole world.'

Even though she may have had some earlier romances, 'I never really had a boyfriend before,' Winona admitted later. At 17, and after a barely worth mentioning two-week fling with her *Heathers* co-star Christian Slater, she hadn't really contemplated or even thought about a serious relationship yet. Not only that, she says, but 'I was no veteran of relationships. It wasn't like I was after Johnny or anything,' she reasoned.

Nevertheless, it looked like it might be fun to pursue. 'I'd heard horror stories about what happens when you dive in real quick.' And she made it clear she wouldn't be diving yet.

She also underestimated the strength of her own emotions. Five months after they met, Johnny gave Winona an engagement ring, and a month later, the couple were living together, even if it was in a succession of hotels and rented apartments. Although Winona soon had him thinking about 'sniffing out a place to own and live. Maybe somewhere on the east coast.'

Not that John Waters, Johnny's soon-to-be director of *Cry Baby*, was convinced. He calls him a homeless movie star. Even after knowing him for a year and a half, he confessed, 'I have a page of addresses for him. The best way to reach him is to write Johnny Depp, A Bench, Vancouver, British Columbia.' Johnny, of course, explained it away by saying, 'I have beds, tables, chairs, a TV set. And they're mine, And I have Winona. That's all I need.'

Johnny Depp and Winona Ryder — it was a relationship made in tabloid heaven. Winona was young, sweet, charming, a child. Johnny, on the other hand, was a hell-raising party monster. Well, according to the press he was. All the same, the gossip columnists couldn't go wrong. Even Timothy Leary would later describe Johnny as both 'wild and charitable', and although Winona focused on the charitable side, the ubiquitous Hollywood insiders found Johnny's apparent past and presumably future indiscretions of considerably greater interest.

There was, for instance, the row of scars that decorated his arms, each commemorating what Johnny deemed an important moment in his life. There was also his own admission that he started smoking at 12, lost his virginity at 13, and by 14 had tried 'every kind of drug there was'. And if that wasn't enough, there was his past record as, one observer put it, 'the kind of passionate fellow who finds scant middle ground between picking someone up and proposing'.

There was also the fact that he had been married and divorced, engaged twice more, and would even spread his engagement to Winona into a trilogy of break-ups and reconciliations, affirmed by the number of times Winona's engagement ring came off and went back again.

And at other times the Irish ring she sometimes wore. The one that, she said, signifies love, friendship and loyalty. Wearing it with the small crown pointing up meant she was taken. But when *Rolling Stone* caught up with her for a May 1989 feature, one month before she spotted Johnny, she was wearing the crown down. 'The longest relationship she had, six months, had just ended because she was away on movie shoots all the time.'

Indeed, it was Johnny's romantic past and presumably future that was the number-one concern. Manhattan was even struck by a brief craze after the announcement of his betrothal to Winona, in which car bumper stickers appeared demanding, 'HONK IF YOU'VE NEVER BEEN ENGAGED TO JOHNNY DEPP'. Not that it bothered him — or did it? 'I'll just answer that I was engaged to Sherilyn, I was engaged to Winona, and I was engaged to Jennifer Grey. But a lot was written about that shit, and it was taken to another level and it was turned into some kind of horrible joke.'

Joke or not, Johnny, of course, had blazed this trail before, pursuing and getting involved with much younger women. His previous engagements as much as his infidelity might well have been his chosen path, but it didn't seem to worry Winona in the slightest, and if it did, she simply shrugged it off. 'People assume it bothers me that he's been engaged before, but it really doesn't. We have a connection on a deeper level. We have the same colouring, but we're from very different backgrounds, so we're interested in each other the whole time.'

Indeed, Johnny had read the Beat poets Winona grew up with, understood the culture that provided the background to her own childhood, and loved to collect the first editions of their work. It was what nourished their appetite for each other, and fuelled their regular weekend visits to the counterculture book store that Winona's father, Michael Horowitz, ran in Petaluma. They also shared a mutual obsession for *The Mission* soundtrack, Jack Kerouac, and J D Salinger's *Catcher in the Rye* — Winona's all-time favourite novel which she said she had read at least 50 times, and affectionately called her personal bible. From that point of view, they shared much more in common than fame.

Not only that but Johnny had never been as involved with a relationship as much as he had with Winona. He even felt the need to set the record straight on his previous liaisons, so widely reported as engagements. 'That's not quite true,' he insisted. 'I was sort of engaged. But if you haven't made some mistakes by 28, it's abnormal. People do whatever they do for whatever reasons, and it's not for anyone else to understand. And basically, it's none of their business.'

Besides, he continues, 'I've never been one of those guys who goes out and screws everything that's in front of him. When you're growing up, you go through a series of misjudgements. Not bad choices, but wrong choices. People make mistakes. We all fuck up. I was really young for the longest time. My relationships weren't as heavy as people think they were. I don't know what it is: possibly I am trying to rectify my family's situation, or I was just madly in love. There's been nothing throughout my 27 years that has been comparable to the feeling I have with Winona. There's something inside me that knows really well, that no one else has ever known, or will ever know. Life is trial and error, but when you find the one who's really it, there's no mistaking it.' That, he explained, was why he was going to get Winona's name tattooed on his arm for $75.

When Winona heard that news, her initial response was excitement and pride. 'I was thrilled when he got the tattoo,' Winona sighed. 'Wouldn't any woman be?' It was only later that her interest turned to apprehension. As she waited at Sunset Strip Tattoo — 'Tattooers of the Stars Since 1971' — while Johnny's 'Winona Forever' double-banner tattoo was engraved into his right bicep to match the tribute to his mother on his left, those feelings grew stronger.

At the same time, 'I was sort of in shock,' Winona freely admits. Besides, 'I'd never seen anyone get a tattoo before so I was pretty squeamish, I guess.' Even as she repeatedly removed the bandage to stare at the engraving that Mike Messina had so perfectly etched, 'I kept thinking it was going to wash off or something. I couldn't believe it was real. I mean it's a big thing because it's so permanent.'

Johnny himself had no doubts. 'I love Winona. I'm going to love her for ever. Putting her on my arm solidified it. The truth is very powerful, believe me this is not something I took lightly.' But according to Messina, 'It was no big deal for him, mainly because he's had tattoos done before.' Even if the process did hurt. But that was all part of the allure. 'Yeah!' Johnny yelped. 'I liked the pain. It was electric, kind of nice.'

Although Winona had already given him a platinum ring, Johnny insisted that rings could be lost. 'Tattoos are extremely permanent.' But would that permanence turn out to be a burden? In expressing his love for her so strongly, Johnny had effectively caged her. Maybe it was then that she realised that on the rare occasion when she did talk about him to the press, the future, their future, never received a mention. Instead, she would talk purely of the present.

The first few months of the couple's life together, however, was spent apart. Johnny was in Vancouver on the set of *21 Jump Street*, while Winona was in Ohio shooting her next role in Jim Abraham's *Welcome Home Roxy Carmichael*. Although work for both would prove to be an aching separation that only long-distance phonecalls and red-eye flights could bridge, it would also provide a welcome rest from the daily harassment of the gutter press. That, of course, didn't stop Johnny's romantic beckoning. One night, he remembers sending Winona 200 helium balloons — 'she could barely walk to the phone to say thank you,' he recalls fondly. They simply 'took up too much room'.

That same summer of 1989, John Waters was looking for an actor to play the part of a delinquent biker in his next project. If there was one thing Johnny had impressed upon his agent, it was how he hated the whole teen idol thing that *21 Jump Street* had imposed upon him. And the best way to get rid of an image, any image, according to Waters, was to make fun of it.

Indeed, *Cry Baby*, or as Waters called it, Elvis Presley's '*King Creole* on acid' was intended as an antidote to all of that. It was a love story about juvenile delinquents set in the mid-Fifties, just before the onslaught of sex, drugs and rock 'n' roll hit the end of that decade.

In fact, the press release described the film as one that lovingly depicts the happiness of teen rebellion and the tragic pitfalls of early conformity in Baltimore of 1954. 'Our Romeo and Juliet heroes are Wade "Cry Baby" Walker (Johnny), a tough, handsome teenage "hep-cat" from the wrong side of the tracks who falls in love with Allison Vernon Williams (Amy Locane), a beautiful rich "square" girl whose raging hormones combined with the evil influence of rockabilly music drive her into the nightmare world of gang mentality and hoodlum passion.'

According to the publicity blurb, the movie, 'with a background of fast cars, gang wars and sexual frustration, would be filled with both original songs and great unheralded music from this forgotten time. John Waters has satirised one of the only movie genres that hasn't been updated in 30 years. Fresh territory for an "historical" black comedy that rips the lid off the throbbing, searing world of yesterday's juvenile delinquents.'

Long before Waters met Johnny, he had already established himself as one of the few independent film-makers with a reputation for what his nickname suggested, the 'Pope of Trash'.

It probably didn't help that in 1972 he had launched Harris Glenn Milstead, an overweight, 300lb transvestite, best known as Divine, for his performance in Waters' own *Pink Flamingos*. The scene where he literally, but unapologetically, chews on fresh dog excrement had the critics virtually stampeding for the exits.

It was, *Variety* noted, 'the most disgusting caper in film history. Surely one of the most vile, stupid and repulsive films ever made.' Nonetheless, it did nothing to tarnish Waters' reputation, nor Milstead's for that matter.

Well, not according to Waters, it didn't. 'He didn't think it was going to hurt his career because at that point he didn't think he was even going to have a career. When he did it, he did it like a professional. He spat it out, brushed his teeth and then got on with his life.' Although 'it was a pretty crazy thing for us to do, it wasn't that crazy,' freely admits Waters today. Mind you, 'I didn't think we'd still be talking about it 25 years later.'

Maybe, too, they would be talking about his next movie 25 years after its release. Perhaps that's why it should be no surprise that Waters would take on a Fifties teen satire. Even if it did end up as a rock 'n' roll musical, *Cry Baby* would still allow the director to shoot what Waters himself would point out was a spoof.

It was, he said, 'a kind of joke on the really wild, untamed youth movies from the early Fifties, except it's the reverse of those movies because the bad guys are who you root for, and the good guys are the villains.'

But with the death of Glen 'Divine' Milstead in 1988, two weeks after the première of *Hairspray*, John Waters had lost his leading lady. 'When he died, there was just no question about having a man dress up as a woman in my films again. There was just no point. Divine was the best.'

Neither could he tell you who he had in mind for the title character of his latest vehicle. Certainly, when he started to think of the who's who among the cream of young Hollywood hopefuls, he simply had no idea. Not to be discouraged, he remembers, 'I went out and bought about 20 teen magazines, which was really mortifying. I found myself hiding them under my jacket. When I got home and started looking through them, Johnny Depp was on the cover of almost every one of them.'

Johnny, Waters was pleased to learn, had the essential attitude about himself, and about his image, to make *Cry Baby* work. 'I think he was very brave to take this part on because, first off, he told me that it was the most peculiar script he had ever seen, and by portraying *Cry Baby*, he would be right out there, making fun of himself.'

As far as Johnny was concerned, though, the whole thing blew him away. '*Cry Baby* came along at a good time for me,' he recalls. 'I had been looking at film ideas for a while and was getting very disillusioned. Most of what I read was flat, just schlock. I was being sent scripts which just echoed what I was doing on *Jump Street*, and I wanted something that would be totally different.'

John, he continues, 'first sent me a letter, and then we talked, and met, and then he gave me a script. I was so excited because not only was it really funny, but it made fun of those clichés and sensitive heroes I had been reading for so long.'

Universal and Imagine Films, the production companies bankrolling the project, were equally delighted. Up to that point, they had only seen one other John Waters movie, and that was *Hairspray*. They were as enthusiastic about that as they were about the script for *Cry Baby*. In their eyes, it was a slick Nineties *West Side Story*.

And they were right, Waters concedes. Even if they were shocked at the sight of Johnny looking the absolute antithesis of the star of the picture. 'He came into this lovely Hollywood office in complete rags,' Waters remembers. And then, 'in the middle of the meeting, he looked at me and gave me a sneer. At that moment, I realised he would do just fine. He understood the whole plot of the film.'

Equally shocked was Waters himself. Not at Johnny, but at the budget for the movie. 'They gave me $8 million to make it,' something the director just wasn't used to. Now for the first time scenes could be laboriously set up over hours of preparation. They wouldn't have to be cut short or abandoned altogether. And the plot, continuous on paper, could be shot at any point of the compass, so to speak, and reassembled later in the edit suite. It was a director's dream.

Johnny agreed. 'For someone who writes and directs, someone who is basically the entire creative force, the real surprise is basically how open John is to ideas and suggestions. He was real accessible, not distant or brooding. He listens to ideas about adding or taking out lines. If I was having a problem with something, he would rehearse me. I mean, he would actually get out there with me. No other director I've worked with has stood there, and danced for me, to help me understand a step.'

At the same time, though, Johnny also recognised another bonus. 'One of the main reasons for doing the movie with John was because it would be contradictory to what everyone sees me as or what I've been labelled as, by some fuckhead with a tie.'

Although Los Angeles singer and songwriter James

Intveld was recruited to vocalise the eleven musical numbers, Johnny, contributing his own footnote to the film's musical score, would consult with the crew on the tiniest of details. Every object on the set from vintage guitars to amplifiers were carefully researched and selected for their authenticity. It was something Johnny was more than qualified to be consulted upon.

But the biggest high for *Cry Baby*, Waters continued, 'was that it was an official selection for the Cannes Film Festival. The midnight screening was completely sold out. Standing ovation. They loved it. Standing at the top of that red carpet and turning around to eight million paparazzi with Ricki Lake and Rachael Talalay, my producer, was a huge high for me. That was a fantasy I wanted since I was 14.'

So, *Cry Baby*, he continues, 'was a good experience for me in the long run. Out of all the movies, it was probably the happiest on the set. There were some problems, but I think people had a lot of fun working on it.'

Johnny certainly did. Especially when Winona visited the set. He particularly enjoyed introducing her to everyone, and even more the considerable presence they had at the première in New York the following April. It was there that Johnny dressed in yellow, and Winona in black, with Johnny's Valentine's gift, an antique gold cross set with rubies on an onyx chain — would be wowing the paparazzi once again. It was also where they would be called the 'bumble bee couple' by much of the tabloid press. Not that it mattered. The reviews for the film were excellent.

Peter Travers writing in *Rolling Stone* said, 'Waters' bad taste is unassailable. The subversive comic thrust of *Cry Baby* shows he simply had to find new ways to channel his baser instincts. The wizard of odd still runs amok.'

Variety, too, supported the film, claiming Waters' 'mischievous satire of the teen exploitation genre is entertaining as a rude joyride through another era, full of great clothes and hairdos. Johnny is great as the delinquent jive, delivering the melodramatic lines with straight-faced conviction and putting some Elvis-like snap and wiggle into his moves.'

Britain's *Sight and Sound* was equally complimentary. 'Johnny Depp is a *bona fide* teen idol.' And London's *Evening Standard* film critic Alexander Walker agreed: 'Genuine heart-throb Johnny Depp is everything a boy should be: young, good looking and mean.'

CHAPTER 6

'Johnny's taste and looks seem in complete
contradiction to Winona's. Everything about
this couple seems very English: debutante girl
meets eccentric Bohemian boy. Their home,
their clothes and the way they are together
are very romantic. Whoever would have thought
that in 1991, it would be hip to be romantic,
but these two are definitely both.'

Vogue

King And Queen Of Kook

December 1989 was the coldest ever recorded in Boston, where Winona Ryder was shooting her subsequent movie role in *Mermaids*. It was also the destination for Johnny's regular cross-country treks throughout *21 Jump Street*'s fourth season, his last, as he travelled back and forth to see her, catching the last flight out of Vancouver every Friday and the last one back every Sunday. 'It was worth it, but man, I was a world-weary traveller.'

That alone was enough to suggest this was a different kind of relationship for Johnny. In fact, it was the closest he would come to actually getting married. Although he openly admitted to relishing the idea, he remained uncertain as to whether or not he believed in the concept. Sure, he liked the image, but still questioned whether one person could be with another until 'death them do part'. He simply couldn't tell if that was humanly possible. All the same, he was prepared to give it a try, and who better to try with, than Winona? 'We'll do it when we have a chunk of time and we can do it quietly with a three-month honeymoon. I've heard about places in Australia, islands where you can be dropped off, and there's nothing there at all. I guess you just run around eating coconuts, foliage and bugs.'

Winona would probably have agreed. 'I've got the feeling that this is right. But I don't want to do it just so I can say I did it. I want to have, like, a honeymoon and the whole shebang. We're going to get married as soon as we have time and we're not working.' In another period, she repeated much the same sentiment. 'Johnny and I have both been working really hard on *Edward Scissorhands*, so we haven't had much time to talk about when the marriage will be. But it will be!'

Even Winona's father was enthusiastic. He himself entertained no doubts whatsoever. If anything, his instincts screamed approval. 'He thinks "Marry him!"' said Winona, taking her evidence from the weekends she and Johnny spent at Winona's family home. Once there, she remembers, they were completely pampered. 'They really love him a lot and even bring me and Johnny breakfast in bed. They're so cool.' Yet it could have turned out so differently. 'It would have been easy not to like me,' Johnny added, 'older people might have just seen tattoos.'

Far less cautious, in fact, was Cher, Winona's co-star from *Mermaids*. She did her best to warn Winona. 'Neither one of them knows what they are doing, but they might as well go through it together. At least she's going through it with a person who cares a lot about her.' Not that Winona disguised her determination. As far as she was concerned nobody was going to preach to her about Johnny. 'She really likes Johnny, so I think she's pretty happy for me,' Winona said of her co-star. 'And although she gives me advice, she doesn't expect me to take it. I'm going to do what I'm going to do anyway.'

The tabloid press, of course, was a different matter entirely. 'We don't feel like royalty,' complained Winona, recalling the time that *People* magazine named them the King and Queen of Young Hollywood. 'We read in the papers when they make that comparison and it makes us giggle. It makes us self-conscious in a way that neither of us enjoys. It's uncomfortable to be watched all the time or to have people eavesdropping on your conversations in a restaurant. They make things up about you which is even worse.'

But according to Daniel Waters, the scriptwriter from Winona's movie *Heathers*, she enjoys it more than she's prepared to admit. 'There's a part of her that likes it even though she denies it. Right now, she's got a Natalie Wood obsession.' Not surprising when you consider that Winona would become the first American actress since Wood successfully to transcend a career from adolescence to adulthood in the full glare of the Hollywood spotlight.

Certainly, she and Johnny would have considerable presence at the ShoWest movie event in Las Vegas where the National Association of Theater Owners saluted them both as the Young Stars of Tomorrow. It was where, with matching rings, they publicly announced their engagement, and according to *US* magazine, acted 'like a couple of teenagers, groping each other and falling to the floor'. But did they really? Even if they did, it was no more than what any other young couple in love and just engaged would do. Still, the press couldn't stop talking about it.

Neither could the Hollywood grapevine. 'When I was young, I was the sweetheart of the press,' acknowledged Winona. 'They loved me, but they were kind of waiting for me to mess up. I had no skeletons in my closet, no major past to talk about. I wasn't with anyone. Then I became engaged to Johnny.'

She had just turned 18 and was still getting acquainted with the tabloids. 'Suddenly people are curious about things you wouldn't even tell your friends.' It was Cher, Winona credits, with helping her through much of that. 'She's been through that her whole life — she taught me what I should take seriously and what I should let go.'

Indeed, it was during this time that Johnny developed his hatred for the press, and Winona carefully began to keep her media exposure in check. Most actors have a love-hate relationship with journalists. Although most are willing to be accommodating with film publicity, when their private lives are under the microscope, most celebrities object to the intrusion. Even when things are stable, being asked the same question 10,000 times is understandably irritating.

It was this aspect that annoyed Johnny more than any other. He particularly remembers one occasion when he was 'in the john of some bar and some stranger came up to me, and said, "So, are you and Winona still together?" At the urinal, for Christ's sake!' Another, *Shout* magazine, went even further, when they pleaded with Johnny to spill the beans on whether he was still, as they put it, 'snogging Winona'!

Neither could he forget just how pernicious the influence of the tabloid press could be. One incident, in particular, had drawn unwanted attention to them both. Winona was due to star in Francis Ford Coppola's *The Godfather Part III* as Mary, the daughter of the Corleone family reprised by Al Pacino and Diane Keaton in the roles they made famous, or had been made famous by, almost two decades before.

It was, recalls Patrick Palmer, Winona's producer from *Mermaids*, an opportunity for her to star in a true American classic that would establish Winona as a genuine adult star, if for nothing other than the love scenes with Andy Garcia. It was something she hadn't really touched upon in her earlier roles, not that she would be participating in any nude, or even semi-nude, scenes for the voyeuristic benefit of the cameras.

Less than a day after Winona finished *Mermaids*, she and Johnny boarded a plane for Rome. Although she was still exhausted from the upper-respiratory problem that had hit her during filming, she was not concerned. Not even as she sniffed and coughed her way across the Atlantic. But almost as soon as they stepped off the plane, they both knew she was in bad shape. She was literally burning up with a 104-degree fever. Not only that, but her lungs were killing her, and the pressurised cabin had made her ears extremely painful. Days later, her condition was exactly the same, but right on schedule, she presented herself for work. Then she collapsed in her hotel room.

Johnny immediately summoned the production team doctor, who promptly announced Winona too sick to work, and too sick even to fly home for a few days. 'I literally couldn't move. It wasn't my choice. It was out of my hands.' Even when she and Johnny did eventually fly back to Petaluma, all she could do was lie in bed. 'I had nothing left in my system. I was a wreck in every sense of the word and I just needed to rest and do nothing.' But as a result, 'I was getting threats that my career would be over and that I was going to get sued,' she recalls. Even her agent warned that if she walked out of the movie she might as well give up acting there and then. Winona left the agency some time later. But what good did that really do? Everywhere she turned, it seemed, the advice was the same.

The press, of course, was another matter entirely. Winona recalls, 'I was sick physically, and exhausted. That's what happened.' But immediately on her return home, and for months to come, Winona became equally sick of having to defend herself. The standard catalogue of absurd and untruthful rumours circulated around Hollywood about why she had left the movie; she was pregnant, she had overdosed, she was having a nervous breakdown, it was drugs, it was an eating disorder, it was Johnny having an affair, it was an assortment of other disasters.

Some even suggested it had been engineered so that she and Johnny could make *Edward Scissorhands* together. What seemed to escape their attention, though, was the fact that Winona had already agreed to appear in the film long before Johnny was cast alongside her. Later, she would concede that the two movies' schedules did conflict, but that was a bridge she intended to cross when she came to it.

Finally losing patience, Winona snapped, 'It's amazing how people want things to be as nasty and complicated as possible.'

The truth, she continued, was simple. 'I was told by my doctor that I couldn't work. I don't know why nobody believed it. Maybe people thought Johnny was influencing me, but he wasn't. He was just taking care of me, ordering room service, sticking his fingers down my throat, helping me to throw up.' Today, Winona credits Johnny alone with helping her through the ensuing storm. But how many times would she have to defend her decision to walk out on *The Godfather*? How many times would she have to explain?

'Sure, it's disappointing, devastating in fact. I wish it didn't happen, but it did. Obviously I would have loved to have worked with those wonderful actors and a great director. But it wasn't a choice. It wasn't like, "Well, I'm not feeling well today. Maybe I won't do this movie." The doctor was there and he said, "You have an upper-respiratory infection. You can't do it." My leaving the movie was a disappointment to everyone. Especially me.'

For the time being though, all Winona could do was lie in bed, and recuperate throughout the period she should have been filming in Rome. She also focused on making sure her relationship with Johnny worked out. But it wouldn't be the only time. 'He is an amazing person whom I have an enormous amount of respect for and very deep feelings for. It's not a possessive, weird little Hollywood promenade.' When she did finally return to work, it would be alongside Johnny on Tim Burton's warm Florida set of *Edward Scissorhands*.

Even in a profession where unconventionality is

often a by-word for success, Tim Burton was never cut out to be a 'typical' Hollywood director. At 29, this native Californian who grew up within earshot of Warner Brothers' massive Burbank lot had erupted on to the scene with his directorial début, Paul Reubens' unexpected hit, *Pee Wee's Big Adventure*. That was five years before he met Johnny, but since that time he had by-passed movies completely only to end up having Hollywood at his feet.

The success of Winona's *Beetlejuice*, with its $73 million dollar gross, and the first *Batman* movie had firmly established him among the upper echelons of Hollywood directors. Although his visions seemed to defy logic, they nevertheless continued to strike a profitable chord with audiences. *Edward Scissorhands*, Burton's peculiar tale of a man-made man with scissors for hands, would prove to be no different. In fact, he ended up with a movie that would eventually gross a respectable $54 million dollars at the box office.

The idea for *Edward Scissorhands* had haunted Burton ever since he was a child, the image living in his mind long before he learned he might be able to bring it to life on celluloid. Through his first years of success, Edward continued to play on the director's mind, until finally, during pre-production on *Beetlejuice*, he commissioned Caroline Thompson to write a screenplay. 'I had read her book, *First Born*, which was about an abortion that came back to life. It was good ... close to the feeling I wanted for *Edward Scissorhands*.'

Nevertheless, it was, according to Thompson, an unusual scripting assignment. 'Tim had the image of this character,' she recalls. 'He said he didn't know what to do with it, but the minute he described it and said the name Edward Scissorhands, I knew what to do. It was Tim who came up with the image of the guy with the hedge-clipper hands and I came up with everything that had to do with them. It was the perfect joining of our talents.'

Originally, the idea was to produce *Edward Scissorhands* as a musical comedy. Thompson even wrote a song, 'I Can't Handle It', but the idea was scrapped in a subsequent revision. Although most of the script remained remarkably similar to the early drafts, it was still a variation of Burton's obsession with the Frankenstein theme.

All the same, he could not explain his fascination with Edward. It was simply 'an image I liked. It came subconsciously and was linked to a character who wants to touch but can't, who was both creative and destructive.' He acknowledged, as Thompson did, that it could have been almost autobiographical, something that 'probably came to the surface when I was a teenager, because it is a very teenage thing. It had to do with relationships. I just felt I couldn't communicate.'

He would work with that same sense of alienation in mind as he set about selecting his cast. Although he agreed to the studio's suggestion that he consider Tom Cruise for the title role, Burton already knew that the *Top Gun* superstar was one of the last people who could capture the bizarre sense of the out-of-the-ordinary that Edward Scissorhands demanded. There were others, of course, equally anxious to try out for the part: William Hurt, Tom Hanks and Robert Downey Jnr. Even Michael Jackson. Not that it mattered. Burton wanted Johnny Depp.

Johnny remembers his first meeting with Tim

Burton very well, mainly because he thought the young, rumpled figure sitting opposite him in the coffee shop of the Bel Age Hotel in Los Angeles looked as if he was in need of sleep. He was, recalls Johnny, 'a pale, frail-looking, sad-eyed man with hair that expressed much more than last night's pillow struggle'.

Johnny, on the other hand, was exactly what Burton had expected. At the time, expounded Burton, 'Johnny was very much known as a teen idol and perceived as dark and difficult and weird and was judged by his looks, but he's almost completely the opposite of this perception. So the themes of Edward, of image and perception, of somebody being perceived to be the opposite of what he is, was a theme he could relate to.'

All the same, Johnny remained uncertain about entering into Burton's world of visionary imagination. In his eyes, he thought, 'I was a TV boy. No director in his right mind would hire me to play this character. I had done nothing workwise to show that I could handle this kind of role. How could I convince the director that I was Edward, that I knew him inside out?'

But did he know him well enough to play the part? It turned out that he did. 'I connected with it really well, I sort of already knew the character and what he represented. Edward seemed more of a feeling than a person. The metaphor of the scissors is about wanting to touch, but if you touch you destroy. Nothing you do seems right. It's the feeling you get when you're growing up, very adolescent. I felt that way. I think everyone did.'

Even after the meeting with Burton, Johnny was not entirely convinced that he would be offered the part. 'My chances were slim at best. Better-known people than me were not only being considered for the role, but were battling, fighting, screaming for it. I waited for weeks, not hearing a thing in my favour. All the while I was researching the part. It was now not something I merely wanted to do, but something I had to do. Not for any ambitious, greedy, actory box-office draw reason, but because this story had now taken residence in the middle of my heart and refused to be evicted.'

When Johnny finally got the call, and the part, he was ecstatic. 'I couldn't fucking believe it.' Burton, he said, 'was willing to risk everything on me in the role. Headbutting the studio's wishes, hopes and dreams for a big star with established box-office draw, he chose me. I became instantly religious, positive that divine intervention had taken place. This role for me was not a career move. This role was freedom. Freedom to create, experiment, learn and exorcise something in me.'

That something was, as Johnny explains, like being 'rescued from the world of mass-product, bang-'em-out TV death by this odd, brilliant guy who had spent his youth drawing pictures'.

The decision to cast Winona was equally instinctive. 'She's the best,' Burton raved. 'She has something you can't even talk about. She's a throwback to movie stars throughout film history. There's something about her skin and her eyes and her ability and her gravity that you can't verbalise. Magical.' For Winona, it wasn't only the chance to work with Burton again, but also with Denise Di Novi, her producer from *Heathers*, and now president of Tim Burton Productions. Later, of course, she learned Johnny was also being approached, but as far as she was concerned that was simply a bonus even if it was a nerve-wracking one.'

'Working with Johnny turned out to be really great, but I was scared and nervous about it. I mean, if there's one person that I want to impress with my acting, it's him. So there was a lot of insecurity during the first couple of days, but it turned out to be a really motivating situation. I think we have pretty good chemistry.'

Johnny agreed. 'The fact that we're together and we're in love certainly won't hurt the movie. But I was nervous. It's like another level of exposing yourself to someone. You know, you can be together, but then to act together, be different people, especially someone like Edward. It was scary at first. She was nervous, too. But it was great. Besides the fact that I love her and everything, she has a lot of talent, she's a great actress, very giving and considerate. It was really easy working with her because stuff automatically happens. You don't have to try. Stuff comes out. I'm sure we're going to do more things together. People have had great success at that, like John Cassavetes and Gena Rowlands. In a perfect world, I'd just do movies with Winona, John Waters and Tim Burton, and live happily ever after.'

Neither did it worry Burton in the slightest that his two stars were in a relationship. He knew Winona too well, and his instincts screamed approval of Johnny. They were, he laughed approvingly, 'kind of an evil version of Tracy and Hepburn'. Indeed, once the filming was over, he confirmed, 'I don't think their relationship affected the movie in a negative way. Perhaps it might have if it had been a different kind of movie, something that was tapping more into some positive or negative side of their relationship. But this was such a fantasy. They were very professional and didn't bring any weird stuff to the set.'

Indeed, to depict a love between such dramatically opposed characters of Edward and Kim was a bold move on Burton's part but a necessary one. He was aiming to disrupt and to upset the viewers preconceptions without alienating them. Just as his stars adapted to roles that were completely contrary to any they had previously played, he hoped his audience would adapt by accepting the unexpected strangeness of Edward and Kim's relationship. Similarly, the film's setting — a slice of Florida suburbia strikingly repainted in bright pastels by production designer Bo Welsch — was selected to convey a sense of startling peculiarity depicted nonetheless as warmly familiar.

Edward Scissorhands wastes no time introducing the world which Edward is about to be thrown into. From the winding suburban development that ends at the foot of a hill dominated by a large, derelict Gothic mansion, Avon Lady Peg Boggs (Dianne Wiest) makes an out of the way call to discover the greatest of secrets: Edward, a boy living alone whose hands are an array of lethal blades. So she does what any normal Avon Lady would do. She takes him home with her to live with her family and, as if to ignite the comedy of errors and misunderstandings that follow, she even boards him in a bedroom with a waterbed.

Although Edward is quickly welcomed into the neighbourhood as a sort of sideshow attraction as he creates a gallery of living sculptures, clipped hedges, spruced lawns, coiffed poodles and even crafted hairstyles for his benefactress and others, his popularity, just as quickly, breeds resentment.

A main reason for this is his obvious affection for Kim (Winona), his hostess's cheerleading daughter, whose increasing awareness of Edward's feelings provokes her jock boyfriend (Anthony Michael Hall) into a succession of bullying outrages. Even the middle-aged seductress (Kathy Bates) whose advances are spurned by Edward soon joins the fray, and as misunderstandings mount, so does the climax of the movie. It begins with a hunt scene lifted, almost unapologetically, from countless Frankenstein pictures. The only real difference is that this time the monster survives, but the affinity, of course, is deliberate.

Equally deliberate was Burton's casting of his greatest cinematic idol, the veteran English actor Vincent Price as Edward's inventor, who doubles up as his father in echoes of Disney's *Pinocchio*, and whose presence in so many Frankenstein movies was so memorable. The two men would subsequently become close friends. In fact, Burton's next project, *Conversations with Vincent*, was a documentary of Price's life, who himself would make no further movies before his death in 1993. While the film remains unfinished and unreleased, *Edward Scissorhands* stands as a fitting tribute to Price's genius.

As much as Burton, Johnny, too, remained close friends with Price up until his death. In fact, he was thoroughly enamoured with him, particularly when the actor would encourage him to shake off the vestiges that typecasting hell could bring — something that had dogged his own career through a string of movies that Johnny considered never less than brilliant.

'One of the greatest things that Vincent Price, a

very, very smart man, ever told me was "buy art". That's a piece of advice I'll treasure for ever.' But where would he keep such treasures? As Johnny confessed at the time, 'I haven't bought a home yet.' Neither did it look as if he was about to.

Even at the height of his fame, he wasn't sure 'if, when I do, it's going to be in the States. It may be in France somewhere. But I have bought a lot of paintings and drawings and some photographs. It's good to have things around that feed you.' One of those things were the original *Edward Scissorhands* scissor hands resting peacefully on a wooden chest at the top of the stairs of Winona's new Los Angeles home she would be sharing with Johnny by late spring 1991.

It was also where, among the mementos and messages stuck to the refrigerator door, there was a photo of Johnny with his *Cry Baby* director and the couple's close friend, John Waters, and a piece of yellow note paper bearing Jason Robard's phone number. He'd been Winona's co-star from *Square Dance*, her first starring movie role. It was Robards, Winona credits to this day, who 'taught me how to be natural in front of the camera'.

Down the line, of course, Burton's creation exorcised demons — both his own and those of his cast. Discussing Johnny's portrayal of Edward, the director remarked, 'I think a lot of the character is him. He has this kind of naïve quality which as you get older gets tested and has holes poked into it. I would imagine Johnny is somebody who would want to protect that to some degree.'

Certainly, a sizeable portion of the movie was devoted to that theme, first in the eyes of the audience when Kim's boyfriend leads Edward directly into trouble with the law, and much more literally, when the boyfriend is killed by the cornered Edward. 'That was probably some sort of junior high or high school revenge fantasy,' Burton confessed. 'Perhaps I was just letting off steam.'

Edward Scissorhands also fascinated the media not only as a movie, but also because of the real life relationship between its stars. Certainly the tenderness between Edward and Kim was derived at least in part from Johnny and Winona's real-life feelings, and several reviewers picked up on that chemistry following the movie's Christmas 1990 release in America, and the following summer in Britain.

Even more intriguing were the hundreds of scripts that Johnny and Winona were sent subsequently. 'They're so obvious,' Johnny noted. 'They offered us a gangster movie. I'm a mobster and Winona's my moll.' There was, however, one idea that Johnny simply adored. *Movieline* had suggested that he try and talk John Waters, his director from *Cry Baby*, into directing him and Winona in a 'whacked-out remake of *Viva Las Vegas* with Johnny taking over from Elvis Presley's hip-swivelling grease monkey, and Winona from the frenzied, lip-smacking Ann Margret'. 'That would be beautiful,' conceded Johnny. 'I would love to do something like that, especially with the Dead Kennedys' version of the theme song.'

All the same, the public perception of Johnny and Winona's relationship was already so troubled that when Johnny and Winona attended a Tim Burton tribute at the Montreaux Film Festival, their presence was described as a notable reconciliation simply because the couple hadn't been seen out for a few weeks. Not together, anyway.

Even Burton was stunned by the posse of paparazzi that were at Los Angeles Airport when he, Johnny and Winona flew back from Florida after completing *Edward Scissorhands*. 'It was one of the most horrible things I've ever seen in my life,' he recalled with contempt. 'I'm sort of a believer that if you're in the public eye you've got to accept a certain amount of that. But I've never seen anything so hostile.'

Winona agreed. 'We got off the plane, and about 50 paparazzi jumped out and started taking our pictures. We couldn't, like, see where we were going because the bulbs were popping. One guy stuck out his foot and tried to trip me! They were yelling at us, trying to get an "interesting picture". Finally, Johnny got so mad that he turned around and flipped them off. Now you'll see his picture in a magazine and he's going to look like some asshole.' Besides, Winona continues, 'aren't we allowed to be in a bad mood sometimes? Everybody else is.'

Indeed, one of those pictures, still unpublished, did exactly what Winona predicted. Even the press copy that went with it did much the same: 'Hollywood has a new Bad Boy. It was shades of Sean Penn [known for his violent temper] as actor Johnny Depp and his fiancée, actress Winona Ryder, arrived at Los Angeles International Airport on a flight from Tampa, Florida. Depp, of Fox TV's *21 Jump Street*, was snapped as he spat at clicking photographers, flung his lit cigarettes in their faces, telling them to 'FUCK OFF!' Clearly embarrassed, Ryder shielded her face with a small piece of luggage, ducked her head and kept walking.'

But that wasn't the only occasion. The papers, cursed Winona, 'were always trying to put me with other people. I mean I work with actors and I know them, and sometimes I might have lunch with them, but that's the end of it. And Johnny does the same thing with actresses. I guess part of it is that they want to get a reaction, and they also want to start a scandal, an affair, or whatever.'

She was right. It was even confirmed when she was allegedly reported to have had a 'very cosy dinner with Christian Slater at the Hard Rock Café in Los Angeles holding hands when they weren't chowing down on their cheeseburgers and fries,' two years after she had ended her two-week fling with the actor. But, Winona snarled, none of that is true.

Neither was the story, on another occasion, when *People* magazine asked HOW DEPP IS HER DEVOTION? after she had been spotted at a Hollywood party with *Dracula* co-star Gary Oldman. According to sources, wrote Mitchell Fink, the pair were 'looking a lot closer than two actors who happen to be making a movie together'.

But Fink continued, 'A source close to Ryder, while acknowledging that Winona is "an affectionate kitten", says Ryder doesn't even like Oldman. "He may have hit on her at one time," says the source, but her relationship with Johnny Depp is "stronger than ever". They have gone through some difficult times, but they are still engaged.'

Although Winona admitted the gossip hurt, 'I don't really read those papers,' she vowed at the time. But she also acknowledged there was no way to avoid finding out what they alleged. 'You hear about it, but you can't pay too much attention because it's too tiresome.' Again, she was right.

Long before all of that nonsense, of course, Johnny

had asked John Waters, now a mail-order minister, to marry him and Winona in Las Vegas. It was the one claim to fame that Johnny was most proud of. 'I'm responsible for having John Waters ordained. I sent off to the Universal Life Church and had him ordained by mail. He's now Reverend John Waters and we want him to perform the ceremony. Who better?'

Who better indeed, but Waters, although enthusiastic, was initially reluctant. 'I told them I wouldn't do it without their parents' blessing. I've met her parents. They've eaten dinner here and I'm not gonna just horrify them.' There were other times when Waters, as he put it, would counsel the couple. 'Too young! I tell them to wait, wait, wait. But, yes, I'd be thrilled to perform the ceremony. I'd feel like the Pope!' There was also another stumbling block. Winona herself. Although Johnny said she loved the idea, when she became the party-pooper and refused to go along with the scheme, it did nothing more than prompt a fresh deluge of stories, this time about jilted grooms and unrepentant brides.

It was if no one could believe Winona might have tamed the wild Johnny Depp. Although he had made no secret of his past liaisons, there never seemed to be a lack of 'close friends' willing to testify that they weren't all in the past. And it only made matters worse when the couple did answer questions about their private life. Did they throw wild parties? Did they go out to the New York nightclubs? Not according to Johnny, who claimed he didn't even know where they were. 'We walk, wander, frolic, then we rent movies and go home.' Just like any other couple. By making stardom sound so mundane, they also moved reporters to dig deeper.

Even when Winona was once asked about her desires for stage work it was no different. If she believed she would be bored with doing the same thing over and over every night, why then did she get engaged at 18? Wasn't that the same thing every night? No, it wasn't. 'And anyway,' she hinted shyly, 'it's definitely not the same thing every night.'

Besides, she continued, 'We're both young, and I think we should be making the most of our relationship at this stage.' But, according to the press, there had to be something else going on, hadn't there? 'I don't know what the obsession is,' condemned Johnny. 'It's so crazy that newspapers make up all these stories about me that never really happened. Part of it is my fault because I spoke fairly openly about my relationship with Nonie.'

Neither was he convinced that his romance with Winona was, as some observers put it, 'treated with kid gloves by casting them as romantic innocents amid all the usual gossip about Bruce Willis and Demi Moore, or Julia Roberts and Kiefer Sutherland'. True, Hollywood had always thrived on celebrity romance, but for Johnny to see his love life diagnosed like a cultural symptom, or publicly consummated and consumed, did nothing more than irritate. But neither could he condemn the fact that, to all intents and purposes, Johnny and Winona were also being packaged as the fairytale couple, a symbol of 'Hollywood Romance'. Even the occasional fashion shoots they did together — embracing and kissing — insisted they were.

Although they weren't short of money, they never blew it on wild excesses. Instead, explained Johnny, 'I like to shop for weird things if I'm with Winona. We found a genie inside an old lamp, and clown posters. Clowns have always scared me, so I think if I surround myself with them, it'll ward off evil.' He even let it slip in one interview that he had a nine-foot cock which raised a few eyebrows. 'I always thought it was good to say that I had the biggest cock in Los Angeles. I am not saying there are no grounds for that without him, but when you have a nine-foot rooster you can say that to anyone.' He had bought that as well, a fibre-glass rooster that he found outside a shop in Hollywood. 'I had to have it. It used to protect me from the clowns.'

As a child, Johnny was horribly aware of his phobia. 'I don't remember one particular incident, I've just always hated them.' His fears were most probably magnified the day he bought a painting of a clown by convicted murderer John Wayne Gacy. 'Before he was caught, Gacy used to go around as Pogo the Clown. Now on death row, he paints clowns, and if you send him a photo, he'll paint you.' It was, as far as Johnny was concerned, 'really sick'.

Less fatefully, of course, were the little gifts and presents Johnny and Winona used to buy each other. For Winona: roses, clothes and jewellery, including her first pearl necklace. And for Johnny: antique locks for his Houdini hobby and first editions of their favourite authors.

There was also the galactic star located in the Northern sky in the constellation Cepheus, not visible to the naked eye, that Winona bought and named 'Jun' after him. Much the same way as you can buy acres of rain forest. Some, however, had seen that as an attempt at a reconciliation. According to Mitchell Fink writing in *People Weekly*, 'A woman in the throes of splitting up does not pay to name a star for her man.' Nor does she pay an extra $44 to get him a framed certificate. Indeed, insisted Johnny, they were simply a young couple still very much in love.

If that was true, then work would again provide an aching separation for both. While Winona contended with her own set of demons on Francis Ford Coppola's *Dracula* shoot, her first role as an adult, Johnny himself was thrown into an equal nightmare on *Arizona Dream*, a movie with a temperamental cast and an even more temperamental director.

Emir Kusturica first came to the Yugoslavian public's attention with 1984's *When Father Was Away on Business*, a documentary study of the national betrayals of Yugoslavia in the Fifties seen through the eyes of a young boy. Five years later Kusturica made his mark at Cannes with his Best Director prize for *The Time of the Gypsies*, and was now firmly committed to the idea of filming the mythical American dream filtered through European eyes.

Indeed, the brainchild of *Arizona Dream* came from David Atkin, a student of Kusturica's film classes at Columbia University. It was, he explained, 'a little piece about a young boy who didn't know what to do with his life. Somehow, I was interested in exploring the declining empire of the car industry in the States, because America is always the country of cars and movies. I saw something similar to what I wanted to do.'

It was the story of Axel Blackmar, a 20-year-old, orphaned after his parents' death in an unfortunate car accident six years earlier in which his uncle Leo was driving and who still hasn't forgiven himself for the fatal crash. Axel, however, has since found contentment living in Manhattan 'where you can see everybody and nobody can see you', and counting fish for New York's Department of Fish and Game. His simple contentment, however, is swiftly interrupted when he is summoned back to his Arizona hometown for Leo's wedding to his 'little posh cupcake', half his age and half his size. It is where Leo begs Axel to be his best man, and where, afterwards, he should remain to learn about being a Cadillac salesman at his uncle's showrooms.

Already in this setting is Paul, Leo's other salesman, who's on hand to show Axel the ropes. But he has other things on his mind — dreams of becoming an actor. He can already recite the dialogue from *Raging Bull*, and even comes up with one of the finest moments in the movie, his confounding impression of Cary Grant running from the crop-duster in Hitchcock's *North By Northwest* without saying a word.

Equally confounding is the manic depressive Elaine Stalker and her oppressed stepdaughter Grace, with whom Axel swiftly becomes entangled. Although Elaine fatally shot her husband (the circumstances aren't too clear), she and Grace blame each other whenever it's convenient.

Grace has also already inherited the state's third-largest copper mine and the two women, bonded more by love and loneliness than hatred, live in a vast Victorian ranch house just outside town. Axel initially is more taken in with the glamorous and sexy Elaine and her dream of building a flying machine than he is with Grace, who never stops talking of suicide and her hopes for reincarnation as a turtle.

The *Los Angeles Times* critic Kevin Thomas would describe the film as 'a dazzling, daring slice of cockamamie, tragi-comic Americana envisioned with magic realism by a major distinctive film-maker'.

With $17 million dollars of French money and two French producers, Claude Ossard and Yves Marmon, Kusturica developed a script for a movie that underwent three title changes from *Arrowtooth Waltz* to *American Dream* to *Arizona Dream*. 'The American dream is the dream of everyone in Western civilisation,' Kusturica insisted. 'To have a car, a little money and a house. But when I was living in America for two years, I found that America itself was very different. People were unhappy and much poorer than I expected. There was a problem then, because in destroying the illusion of the American dream you are also destroying part of your youth, a childhood spent watching movies.'

Johnny agreed. 'I was thrilled to work with Kusturica because I saw *Time of the Gypsies* and it was one of the greatest things I've ever seen.' Not only that, but Johnny applauded the idea of working with yet another director not yet established in the upper echelons of Hollywood, and one, he thought, who would be more open to exploring and experimenting with his material.

He also saw something in the script of which even Kusturica was not probably aware. The role, Johnny notes enthusiastically, was another offbeat oddball taking a unique path in life. Something Johnny himself could relate to, in retrospect, at least. From that point of view, Johnny's fascination with Axel Blackmar should not have been surprising. It has since proven characteristic of his favourite kind of role.

'There's a part of me that always wanted to change. For example, ever since I was a kid, I was fascinated by the idea of time travel, of being someone else in another time. I think that's probably a normal thing. Well, let's hope it is. What interests me is that so-called "normal" society considers them outcasts or on the fringe or oddballs. With any part you play, there is a certain amount of yourself in it.'

There has to be, he reasoned, 'otherwise, it's just not acting. It's lying. That's not to say that I feel different than others. Maybe they have a more difficult time saying "I don't feel accepted" or "I feel insecure". These characters are passive; I see them as receivers. I've identified with them since I was very young.'

Certainly, that was the opinion of the star names rushing to try out for the other parts. Jerry Lewis, a veteran of 17 Dean Martin movies was cast as Uncle Leo; Faye Dunaway and Lili Taylor were recruited to play the mother and daughter team, Elaine and Grace Stalker; and Vincent Gallo, the Seventies underground musician and accomplished painter from New York accepted the part of Paul Blackmar.

All the same, filming itself, on location in Alaska, New York and Arizona, placed a lot of pressure on Kusturica's shoulders. As he himself would later point out, he suffered what he called a nervous breakdown.

Not surprising really. After weeks of exhausting night shoots, escalating budgets, an increasingly erratic cast and looming money-men, he upped sticks and returned to New York, refusing to shoot any more footage of the uncompleted film until his backers would give him more time, more space and more money to realise his vision.

Such antics are generally known as the amorphous creative differences which scupper so many other Hollywood projects. Most films would have seen the director replaced and the movie completed, but the producers swiftly discovered that Kusturica had the cast, including Johnny, right behind him. Indeed, the entire cast and crew refused to consider continuing with anyone other than Kusturica.

'I'm a European director,' he snapped, 'not an American and I just wasn't ready for what they throw at you. They don't want imagination. They want a beginning, a middle and an end, with the end nice and convenient and happy.'

Although Kusturica freely acknowledged that his bizarre all-or-nothing approach led to most of the problems, he was not prepared to acknowledge defeat. 'I don't know what's the matter with me. Perhaps I'm just crazy, but I have this vision and I just have to complete it, no matter what the cost. I'd hate to be my producer.' With *Arizona Dream*, he said, 'I thought I was going to die at least twice. It's too much of a strain.'

Even Vincent Gallo observed the scenes of the dramas that were going on behind the cameras. But he also noted a change in Johnny, too. He had apparently re-invented himself since the two first met on the set of *21 Jump Street*. He was, Gallo recalls, dating Winona, and they were wearing thrift shop clothes for the first time. 'He was tattooed and earringed and on a TV show. I just hated them.'

There were even rumours of a conflict between the two. Their friendship, it seemed, was under strain during the making of the movie. Johnny, he explained, had found a soulmate in Emir Kusturica and constantly demanded his attention. 'And he was not completely nice to me to get it,' Gallo recalls. 'He had this need to be heavily involved with Kusturica. It was almost like a love affair. Emir and Johnny carried around Dostoevsky and Kerouac books and wore black. They had never worn black in their lives.' Not only that, continues Gallo, but 'they kept everybody in the cast and crew awake all night, because they were blasting music and getting drunk.'

The tragedy of Johnny Depp, Gallo continues, 'is that the exterior, the TV pop star turned bad boy, waif lover, hipster friend of Jim Jarmusch, is totally uninteresting. It's tragic that he has this poser part of himself, that he has to invent himself like that. If only he would allow himself to be who he really is, somebody who's traumatised and trapped by his childhood and emotional life, then he would be interesting, a great person, a great talent. He is one of the most funny, talented, likeable, sweet, authentic people I've ever met.'

All the same, Gallo felt no reservations about Johnny's on-screen ability. If you want to see Johnny's greatest moments on film, he insisted, 'look at the scenes where he has no dialogue. He is the most brilliant listener in a movie. There's a scene where we're at a movie theatre and they're showing *Raging Bull*. All he's doing is watching me hustle these girls. I'm telling her we can make love but do not touch my face or my hair, and I start rambling on. "Do you think anybody touches Brando's face? Touch Pacino's face? Does anybody touch De Niro's face? Does anybody touch fucking Johnny Depp's face?" I said, "Do you think fucking Johnny Depp lets anybody touch his face?" I just said it.

'I was goofing because I thought we were just shooting a rehearsal. Johnny is flawless in the scene. He's just brilliant in the scene, he doesn't flinch. I say his name in the scene and he doesn't flinch. He blows me off the screen, and it's my most animated scene in the film.'

There were, of course, other demons Kusturica needed to contend with as the *Arizona Dream* shoot rolled on. Tantamount among these was his relationship with Faye Dunaway. What had started out as a genuine respect for each other became more difficult. It probably didn't help that Kusturica didn't seem to be as attentive towards Dunaway as he was Johnny.

Whatever the reason, it appears the tension between the two was enough to ignite the difficulties, 'But,' Kusturica said, 'we overcame that problem together. I said to her that this is a movie where all the people must act together with each other all the time. If you have any problems, just let me know.' She did that as well. But, admitted Kusturica later, 'she will be very good in the movie.'

In Elaine, agreed *The Detroit News*, 'Dunaway in particular has found one of her most challenging roles as an extremely mercurial, outrageous woman with an image of a crazed nymphomaniac whose vulnerability and longing actually express an acute perception.' Much the same as they said about Jerry Lewis. 'He also gives a serious, endearing performance of one of the most normal men he has ever played.'

And that is what Kusturica had expected from him. Aside from his acclaimed performance in Martin Scorsese's *The King of Comedy*, Lewis hadn't worked that much in movies of late. 'I had heard a lot of bad things about Jerry,' Kusturica smiled. 'But they must have been lies. For me, Jerry was crazy, and extremely pleased because I was laughing at what he did, but at the same time, I had to control him, because in this movie he is dying and had many serious scenes. He is a very good actor. The reason that the cast is electric somehow relates to the States and even to the movies, to things like Jerry's comedies.'

It was something Kusturica learned when he and Johnny left for Cannes to promote the then unfinished movie. All the same, it was a trip that Vincent Gallo believes was as much for Johnny's ego than the purpose of selling the film to distributors. 'Johnny had this need to go to Cannes, and stay at the Hotel du Cap, and then refuse to do interviews — perhaps he had read in an article that Brando refused to do interviews.'

Even when the film did finally make it out to the screens, the expected wide release was as disappointing as the bemused critical reaction following its international début. It won the competition prize at the Berlin Film Festival in 1993, and two years later it received a limited British release in art houses.

Still, Kusturica was not concerned. If anything, it only cemented his determination to work with Johnny again. Unconfirmed rumours began to circulate linking the two together for a modern version of *Crime and Punishment*, set this time in modern-day Brooklyn, but the project apparently fell through when Kusturica's potential Italian backers Penta shut down their failed American operation.

CHAPTER 7

'It was a really good thing that it ended,
I think, for both of us. I don't know how
much the media had to do with it, because we
really had drifted apart a long time before the
press found out that it had ended. So it was old.
I think he's great, and I have nothing but kind
things to say about him, but it was just over.'

Winona Ryder

What's Eating Johnny Depp?

By April 1993, it seemed that Johnny's life with Winona was ending. It had been for over a year. They rarely saw one another any more, and although they kept up appearances when they went out, they didn't go out that much. It was apparent that they had begun to drift apart. They may have shared the same home, but they didn't share the same life. It was just the beginning of what would be a painful end to Hollywood's fairytale romance.

Making matters worse was the difficulty they found in maintaining a relationship amidst successful careers and punishing work schedules that kept them separated much of the time. Constant rumours that they had both been stepping out with other young stars continued to add fuel to the fire. And although they ignored the gossip, refusing to even dignify the tales with a response, the stories still persisted, sometimes even touching on accusations of sleeping with their co-stars, rowing furiously, and not even being together any more.

One of those occasions was while Winona was filming *The Age of Innocence*, Martin Scorsese's adaptation of the Edith Wharton novel, in New York, and Johnny was at home writing a movie with his brother, Dan.

According to insiders, Winona and Daniel Day-Lewis had apparently struck up a close friendship. 'She and Dan Day-Lewis were mad for each other all through the production. It was like a freeing of the soul.' But then again, 'Winona was in love with just being there. She had such a good time. She had so much energy.'

It probably didn't help matters when Day-Lewis revealed how they would sing together. Winona's most impressive number he told the *New York Post* was 'I'm Just a Girl Who Can't Say No'.

Inevitably, headlines soon suggested as much when the film was finally released. Several reviewers picked up on the chemistry between the co-stars, suggesting that their relationship was not just confined to the screen following the movie's release five months after Winona and Johnny had split.

Even if the speculation had been true, and according to Winona's publicist it wasn't, what most failed to acknowledge was the fact that Winona and Johnny were no longer a couple. They hadn't been for at least a year, long before filming started.

On the other hand, Johnny himself apparently wasn't

quite so blameless. According to Tally Chanel, a B-movie actress who had met Johnny at the Hollywood première of Bruce Willis' *Die Hard 2* in July 1990, she said she almost got the opportunity to marry him.

Not only that, but according to some, they dated for a year by spending quiet nights at Johnny's Hollywood Hills home ordering in food from a Chinese restuarant. If that was true, and it probably wasn't, the fact that he was engaged to Winona at the same time didn't seem to matter. Neither, apparently, did his confession that 'he sort of had a crush' on Patty Hearst when they came together on the set of John Waters' *Cry Baby*.

Not that Waters would agree. 'Johnny's a serial monogamist if anything. He's been with very few women since I've known him and for long periods. And he's been very faithful to his women so he's hardly a womaniser.'

Whatever the reasons, Winona was clear about where she laid most of the blame for the eventual collapse of her romance with Johnny. 'I remember us desperately hating being hounded. It was horrible and it definitely took its toll on our relationship. Every day we heard that we were either cheating on each other or were broken up when we weren't. It was like this constant mosquito buzzing around us.'

The end of their romance, of course, was dutifully reported in the press. 'Stick a fork into the relationship of Winona Ryder and Johnny Depp, and you will discover it's done,' wrote *People Weekly*. 'Ryder's representative confirms, after months of press speculation, that Ryder and Depp are a couple no more. The two young movie stars have called off their engagement and gone their separate ways.'

Even Winona's diary entry at the time revealed that

she was feeling 'fragile, a little confused, heartachy and a little tired'. As for Johnny, 'He's a special guy. I was just really young. I don't know what his excuse is, but that's mine.' But whatever she said in public, she still looked for ways to relieve her private agony of the break-up.

'I attempted being an alcoholic for two weeks,' she would smile later, remembering all the nights 'in my hotel room, drinking screwdrivers from the mini-bar and smoking cigarettes' while the doleful sounds of Tom Waits' *Nighthawks at the Diner* album played over and over on the stereo.

For a time, the drinking may have helped, but the night she passed out with a lit cigarette still burning between her fingers, she awoke with a start, drenched in sweat, and suffocating from the fumes that now filled the room. Even as she blinked her way into wakefulness, surrounded by flames and smoke, she was terrified. But it wasn't the fear alone. It was also the thought of what could have happened had she not stirred into consciousness at that moment. 'It was my wake up call,' she says today. It was also enough to ensure she didn't touch the mini-bar again. Besides, she knew that the dizzy oblivion of alcohol was no solution for confronting the painful feelings she felt over the ending of her relationship with Johnny.

Johnny, however, believed his relationship with Winona slowly unravelled over time, the pressure of their film careers, and being constantly hounded by the press taking its final toll. In June 1993, he announced publicly, 'We split up a month ago. When you're with someone and you love them, it's never easy to cut the string, to sever the connection. But, with us, it just came to seem the natural thing to do — a natural progression, just something that had to happen. I wouldn't say that our splitting was exactly a devastating experience for either of us really. We're still friends. We still talk. And everything's fine, very amicable, very nice.' But was it?

As much as Winona was devastated, Johnny was inconsolable. A friend confided anonymously to *People* magazine that 'he was so desperately in love with Winona, that when they broke up, he wouldn't admit that it was over for the longest time.'

Johnny and Winona had started out their life together by being open with the press in the hope that it would satisfy their demand for celebrity news and gossip and finally leave the couple alone, but that did not happen. 'It's very hard to have a personal life in Hollywood,' revealed Johnny at the time, explaining that the decision to be as open as they were was, in fact, a mistake.

'I thought it would destroy the curiosity monster. Instead it fed it. I had nothing but bad luck after talking about this stuff. It became such a public thing. Everyone felt like they were part of it, or owned part of it, or that they'd somehow got the right to ask me about her. I hated it.'

Although Winona filed away her engagement ring along with her other memories, for Johnny the visible tokens of his love for Winona were going to prove far more difficult and far more painful to dispose of. Having seen his 'Winona Forever' tattoo become the object of many an interviewer's questions, and the butt end of as many comedians' jokes over the next year, he began to have second thoughts about removing it.

'I think of my tattoos like a journal and to have it

removed, or erase it, is to try and say it never happened. We were together for three years and at the time, I really did think it would be forever. If I alter it in some way, make it funny, put her next boyfriend's name on top of it — that would be honest.' Over the next year, however, Johnny acknowledged that he was, in fact, going to have it removed.

Even if taking it off would hurt more than putting it on? Johnny agreed. 'Especially if they don't give you the anaesthetic. But it's worth it, the pain going on and off. They're both worth it.' One journalist caught it shortly after the treatment began. 'At the moment, it reads "Wino Forever". And still does to this day.

When asked, Winona felt there was little to be done about the tattoo. 'What do you want me to say? It's like, "It's there, oh well". If I hated him, I'd probably say something poignant. He's a great guy, but I don't really think about it.' Johnny, of course, was less reticent on the subject of the ending of the relationship. Where had all the rebel love gone? He had no idea.

'It's one of the mysteries of everybody's life. It's not like you suddenly go, "You know what? I just don't love you." She's a sweet kid, man, and it's always a little weird. We used to do this and that, and we used to have fun and hang out together. But at least we were able to feel that for each other. I feel real lucky that we got that.'

All the same, *GQ* magazine wondered if they were simply too young and gorgeous to be left alone by the tabloids. 'They kept doing their ridiculously romantic things. She bought him a star. He tattooed her name on his body. It was more than romantic. It was reckless.'

And maybe they were right. Nonetheless, Johnny

didn't relish the thought of being alone again after such a long relationship. Being lonely, he confessed, was scary. 'I've been lonely many times.'

People Weekly, meanwhile, was quick to notice that Winona did not remain alone for long. 'We hear from other sources that Ryder is now seeing David Pirner, lead singer of the rock group Soul Asylum. Pirner apparently left his girlfriend of 11 years to be with Ryder.'

Although the relationship threatened to be as well documented as her previous one with Johnny, and although Winona was not screaming her business from the top of the Hollywood Hills, it was immediately apparent that she felt much more comfortable talking about her relationship with Pirner than she ever did discussing Johnny. 'Our relationship is different from any I've ever had,' she explained. 'It's more casual, it's more of a friendship, really. What I'm basically saying is that it's not full of drama.'

From the pain and turmoil of his relationship ending with Winona, Johnny moved into shooting *Benny and Joon*, a movie based on a screenplay by Barry Berman and Leslie McNeil. The two men had first discussed the project in the early 1980s when both were up-and-coming scriptwriters. A decade later, their passion for the story remained unabated.

Berman, of course, was suitably qualified to pen the story in the first place. He had, after all, been a graduate of Ringling Brothers and Barnum & Bailey's highly competitive Clown College in Florida, earned his apprenticeship in the world-renowned circus, and had loved watching reels of Buster Keaton and Charlie Chaplin's silent comedy classics in between performances under the big top. More importantly, it was what influenced him to create the character of Sam for *Benny and Joon*.

In fact, Berman's screenplay had come to the attention of Susan Arnold and Donna Roth in late 1989. 'Someone told us about this screenplay by Barry Berman, a young, relatively unknown screenwriter,' recalls Arnold. 'The first time Donna and I read the script we could both see that it was filled with jewels. It was simultaneously funny, romantic and poignant. Both of us felt passionate enough about this project to get it made.'

Not only that, but Arnold could also identify with the character of Joon. The producer had previously worked with Imagination Workshop, a California-based arts programme that worked with underprivileged and disenfranchised people as well as with psychiatric patients. 'My experience with the workshop certainly peaked my desire to make a movie about someone who had a little harder time in life than most of us.'

It was the theme that lies at the heart of the movie. The story centred on Juniper Pearl, Joon for short, a smart and talented, but emotionally unbalanced, young girl, who was cared for by her irrepressible, seemingly unselfish, car-repairing brother, Benjamin, or Benny, ever since their parents had died in a fatal car accident.

Joon paints and reads, has a passion for fire and nudging her housekeepers into retirement as Benny works his car clinic, plays poker, and gives up any hope of a serious relationship because he has no idea of how Joon is going to fit in.

The natural order and occasionally clichéd creakiness of this life is suddenly shattered, however, when, at a poker game, Joon loses her hand and wins her opponent's cousin

Sam, a beguiling and whimsical misfit, who at 26 can't even read, spends all day polishing plastic forks, stays up all night watching old movies on TV, and when he does sleep, it's under the sink.

He, of course, charms his way into Joon's heart with his silent comedy capers, does the housework and listens to the rock music blasting from the radio even when it incurs Joon's wrath.

That is enough for Joon to throw him out, as she puts it, 'for cleaning the house'. He, of course, returns with Benny's blessing and Sam's promise to look out for his sister. Not so blessed, as far as Benny is concerned, is the gentle romance that begins for Sam and Joon. Although they are seen simply as two outcasts enjoying each other's company, they are also deadly serious. Serious enough to tell Benny at least. After all, for Joon, Sam offers the only stable love and sweetness she has seen in her troubled world. Their confession, of course, hits Benny like a ton of bricks, who in turn swiftly condemns the affair and in a moment of rage throws Sam out. This time for good.

Complicating matters even further is Benny's admission that he has been considering a placement in a physchiatric home for Joon. Joon leaves after a fight with her brother, joins up with Sam and catches a bus out of town, and out of Benny's life. But Joon can't really cope with the outside world, least of all the claustrophobic confinement of the bus and, as a result, she hurls herself into a state of emotional turmoil.

She is rushed into a psychiatric unit from which, it appears, she may never be released. Benny, however, is so overcome with despair that he even dismisses Sam's offer of help. Matters worsen, however, when the hospital confirms its refusal to release Joon, or even to allow Benny to visit with her. Distraught and helpless, Benny turns once again to Sam for help. After another round of Keaton-style capers to extricate her, Joon returns to live again with Benny as he begins to understand her needs as much as he does his own.

Strangely enough, Johnny was not the first choice for the role of Sam even though he had, for some time, thought it was perfect for him. Unfortunately, a lot of critics completely disagreed. They thought he was in danger of pushing himself into a corner with his odd choice of roles, and any calculated attempts to shake off his oddball typecasting was, as far as they were concerned, less than satisfactory.

Johnny, too, asked much the same. 'Do I search out the weirdest thing I can find and then do it just because it is the weirdest thing I can find?' No, he didn't. 'I just do the things that I like. I have to admit, however, that what I like does tend to be left-field.'

Besides, he continued, 'I feel somehow much more comfortable playing it. I relate more easily than I do when I run across straight roles. I hate the obvious stuff, I just don't respond to it.'

Although Johnny did not share his critics' doubts, they still questioned whether it was a movie for him. The character he would be playing could easily have been taken out of any Buster Keaton silent comedy. Perhaps it's not surprising that he had been flirting with the idea of playing Charlie Chaplin in Richard Attenborough's biopic, the one that had linked Winona Ryder to the project in the role of Chaplin's third wife Paulette Goddard. And that could possibly have been why he turned down the role. After all, it would have turned out to be a very different experience from the one when the couple worked together on *Edward Scissorhands*. As Winona herself would point out, 'I'd work with Johnny again, but right now it might be awkward.'

All the same, continues Johnny, 'I wasn't really a contender for Chaplin. I met with Richard Attenborough, knowing I was totally wrong for the part. I just wanted to meet him. I knew right from the start that I was not right for the role, not physically right, I mean. Robert (Downey Jnr) was the perfect choice. He kind of looks like Chaplin and he's built more like him.'

Certainly that was true, but in any event Johnny saw no cause to regret his decision to accept the role of Sam. It was a perfect alternative to the Chaplin part. More importantly, it offered him the opportunity to work with Jeremiah Chechik, a Canadian-born director not yet established in the Hollywood A-list, and one who probably wouldn't enforce the restrictions that an established director might. It was something that had haunted Johnny ever since working with Oliver Stone on *Platoon*. And one that had caused him to question his own performance as a result.

Chechik also loved the script and, more importantly, the characters. He understood that the moment he read it. 'In the most simple way, it's a romance between two oddities who meet and fall in love.' The story, he observed, 'is universal because every human heart contains the potential for both pain and pleasure. It has a fable quality to it, but it's also very believable.'

He also knew that Johnny would be equally believable. How could he not be? When the two first met, he understood that even more. But he also 'began to understand how much he had brought to the role of Edward Scissorhands. He is so emotionally expressive, doing what seems to be so little. It was clear that he would bring a thoroughly original and exciting energy to the role of Sam.'

Johnny, though, wasn't the only cast member to end up as second, or even third choice. For a while, Chechik sought Tom Hanks for Johnny's role of Sam, and Julia Roberts for Joon. Not surprising, really, since they were two of the hottest names in Hollywood at the time. But when the idea of Hanks and Roberts fell through, the studio, MGM, simply told Chechik to look to casting real-life Hollywood couple Tim Robbins and Susan Sarandon who had already starred together with great success in Kevin Costner's 1988 baseball comedy *Bull Durham*. But that didn't work out either. Eventually, they settled on Johnny for Sam; Laura Dern for Joon; and the still relatively new, affable bartender from *Cheers*, Woody Harrelson, as Benny.

Shooting was already scheduled to get under way in June 1993 when two of the trio quit the production. Dern, who had by now secured an Oscar nomination for her role in 1991's *Rambling Rose* was not prepared to accept third billing below the two male leads, and Harrelson was already in negotiation with director Adrian Lyne to secure the hotly-contested role of Demi Moore's husband in Robert Redford's starring vehicle, *Indecent Proposal*.

As far as MGM were concerned, Harrelson was in breach of his contract and was seriously delaying the production of a major motion picture, and the studio intended to make him aware of that. The actor was promptly sued for $5 million dollars and threatened with an injunction if he were to play any other roles throughout the period he should have been filming *Benny and Joon*. To complicate matters further, Harrelson countered with a claim that he couldn't work with Chechik.

MGM, however, were not convinced and their lawsuit contained what they believed to be the true circumstances behind Harrelson's departure. 'Sudden success has caused Harrelson to attempt to take advantage of his new popularity by disregarding his existing obligation in favour of another motion picture project he now considers more favourable.' Eventually, though, Harrelson's gamble paid off, and he did play the role of Moore's architect husband David Murphy in Lyne's blockbuster movie.

Aidan Quinn, still a couple of years away from Brad Pitt's *Legends of the Fall*, and Mary Stuart Masterson, of *Fried Green Tomatoes* fame, were quickly recruited to fill their places as the remainder of the cast was also assembled. Julianne Moore accepted the part of waitress Ruthie, Benny's would-be love interest. Other roles were filled by CCH Pounder as Joon's counsellor Dr Garvey; and Oliver Platt, Dan Hedaya and William Burch as Benny's pals.

Chechik's final choice of casting Quinn as the protective, straight-laced brother may have been an unconventional one but also proved to be the right one. 'Benny's got the weight of the world on him,' explained Quinn. 'He's the mud of reality, while the others are the sprites of magic. My character is very much a straight man.'

Masterson, on the other hand, would admit that her role was one of the most intriguing she had ever taken on. Not only that but the first day on the set, 'my husband and I had just split up, and I was in the hysterical funk you get in when you're trying to be pulled together. But when Johnny walked in, the energy in the room changed. There's something really amazing about him, his generosity of spirit.'

All the same it was, she confirmed later, 'really revealing to play a character whose confidence is shaken by the confusion she lives with everyday. My own insecurities came right to the surface as a result. But this story is basically about love. There are circumstances that are universal in this story, such as learning how much you can love someone and still allow them to be free.' It was that theme, she said, that lies at the heart of the movie.

Nonetheless, it was not an easy role to prepare for, as much for Johnny as Masterson. As with *Edward Scissorhands*, the role of Sam demanded that Johnny interact not only emotionally but also physically with his character. An on-set mime artist, magician and silent film buff, Dan Kamin, was recruited to coach and choreograph the comedy routines of the screen legends that were all part and parcel of Sam's character. Johnny was thankful for his help as he consulted with Kamin on the tiniest of details. 'He gave me some pointers on movement,' Johnny explained. 'I enjoyed the slapstick part of the movie, although I sustained some injuries.'

Johnny's research was augmented by watching the silent movies of the period — especially the Keaton and Chaplin stuff. 'Since Sam's brand of comedy is physical rather than verbal, in much the same way as silent film heroes, we concentrated on a style of movement,' Kamin explained. 'We started with magic tricks, using sleight of hand and worked our way up to recreating Keaton's patented falls. The subtle movements are the hardest to capture, but Johnny did a marvellous job. He was really courageous and worked hard, even at the small things.'

In one memorable review, the *Mail on Sunday* critic Tom Hutchinson summed up the general critical opinion when he credited Johnny as 'the clowning minder to a mentally ill girl, Depp tenderly reinforces the role of eccentric outsider which has become his province. Delightfully played, it is a fable with potential to touch the heart.' The *Spectator* agreed, remarking how Johnny was 'curiously serious and not so much simple-minded as innocent in *Edward Scissorhands* and *Cry Baby*, and he is all those things again here, and charming. The charm is not forced.' Certainly that was true. In the end though, *Benny and Joon* was a delightful movie.

Although the London *Evening Standard* had called *Benny and Joon* 'too kooky for words', Johnny was not concerned. 'I don't think I'm limiting myself, because I'm doing things that are true to me. I see these characters as much more normal than what's considered normal. There seems to be this constant theme in the things that I do which deal with people who are considered "freaks" by so-called normal people. I guess I'm attracted to these off-beat roles because my life has been a bit abnormal. The only thing I have a problem with is being labelled.'

And he laughed, because that yearning could also be read as a justification of Johnny's next role, the title character in Lasse Hallstrom's *What Eating Gilbert Grape?*, a movie based on Peter Hedges' 1993 novel.

It was the story of the title character who looks after his mother, brother and two sisters in the home that their father built just before he was 'hung out to dry' 17 years earlier in Endora, 'where nothing ever much happens, and nothing much ever will'.

Mama used to be the 'prettiest gal in these parts' but is now a 600lb mountain of a woman who hasn't stepped outside the front door in at least seven years and whose oversized proportions play havoc with the infrastructure of the house they still live in.

Gilbert's younger brother Arnie is mentally impaired and was never expected to survive much beyond childhood, and may not much longer. In fact, it could be any day now. 'Sometimes you want him to live. And sometimes you don't.' His older sister Amy is a home-maker who yearns for normal domestic bliss while the youngest, Ellen, has just turned 15 and had her braces removed.

Gilbert's troubles, however, stretch far beyond his family, extending to his friends, employers and customers. He works at Lamson Groceries which is battling against the huge Foodmarket where everyone else shops on the outskirts of town; he's having an affair with Mrs Betty Carver; and his best friend, Tucker, is going crazy about the opening of a franchise burger joint, the best employment opportunity, he thinks, to hit Endora since, well, since he can remember.

Into this self-contained world bursts Becky and her mother, caravanning tourists who find themselves stranded in the dead-end town for a while with mechanical problems. It is where Becky is forced to involve herself with community life during her brief stay and, of course, Gilbert. At the heart of the movie, though, is Gilbert's indecision — whether to remain loyal to his family responsibilities, or whether to pursue his own freedom for happiness — in the shape of Becky.

Either way, Gilbert is stuck in Endora, explained Hedges of his scripted screenplay. 'He's working in a grocery store and everybody's gnawing at him; his family, his friends, his lover. But into town rolls a girl who collides with everything that has been closed up inside him.'

Indeed, Hedges' novel had only been published for a few days when Swedish director Lasse Hallstrom, best known for 1985's *My Life As a Dog* and more fatefully as the director who had quit Winona's 1990 movie, *Mermaids*, started calling.

That was, Hedges recalled, 'One of my favourite films. I realised that Lasse could bring great humanity to these characters where another director might make fun of them.' Not only that, but when Hallstrom announced who he had in mind for the title role, he was even more excited. 'Gilbert is very much an observer, a reactor in the movie, and Johnny Depp was the perfect actor,' Hallstrom said at the time. 'He has the sensitivity that Gilbert Grape needs.'

Hedges agreed. He had already watched Johnny's performances in *Edward Scissorhands* and *Benny and Joon*, and instantly knew the choice was the correct one. 'He has an almost burning desire to make ugly choices. He comes with a physical beauty that's just astonishing, and at the same time he has no interest in being that. When I met him he had this really long hair and showed up at the meeting, very quiet, really shy, and was teaching us magic tricks. I thought, I suppose he could be Gilbert.'

As Johnny slipped into his character he knew 'Gilbert Grape had to leave his dreams behind because of circumstances. He has a hostility that he can't express because of his duties and responsibilities to his family. To be able to deal with himself everyday, he's had to make himself sort of numb so that he's not affected too much by everything.' Far more important to his portrayal, Johnny concedes, was the fact that 'there were things that have happened in my life that parallel things in Gilbert's life'.

For Johnny, playing the small-town son who takes care of his mother and retarded brother was, in many ways, a throwback to his own childhood; his parents' divorce, looking after his heartbroken mother, and picking up the support cheques from his father. 'It's always taxing to play something that's close to reality, but sometimes you play roles that are close to you. You identify with the guy. Not that you become the person, because I don't buy into that shit at all.'

What he did buy into, however, was the emotional upheaval of not being with Winona any more. Although it does not appear to have affected his performance, he did openly admit that it was one of the most difficult times he ever had on a movie. 'I poisoned myself constantly; drinking, didn't eat right, no sleep, lots of cigarettes. It was really a lonely, really fucking, lonely time.'

All the same, Johnny immersed himself in the role without hesitation. He even had his teeth bonded and chipped. On set, he vowed, he would dye his hair trailer-park red in homage to his friend Bones who had courageously beat out the flames that had set the actor's face alight back in his teens.

In the same way, Johnny elaborates, 'Gilbert would seem like a pretty normal kind of guy, but I was interested in what was going on underneath, in the hostility and the rage that he has and that he's only able to show a couple of times in the film. I understand that feeling of being stuck in a place, whether it is geographical or emotional. I can understand the rage of wanting to completely escape from it and from everybody and everything, you know, and start a new life.'

From that point of view, it is not difficult to appreciate the appeal of the film or the character. It was, Johnny said, 'like Gilbert at some point or another allowed himself to die inside, slowly kind of killing or martyring himself for his family, becoming a surrogate father — even to his mother. That kind of loyalty may start out as pure love, but it can work against you, with love and devotion turning into resentment and guilt and losing yourself, which is the worst thing anyone can do — because then you hate others because of what you have done to yourself.'

Equally instinctive as choosing Johnny for Gilbert was the choice of Leonardo DiCaprio as his mentally handicapped brother Arnie. 'I needed someone who wasn't good looking,' recalls Hallstrom. 'But of all the actors who auditioned for the role, Leonardo was the most observant.'

He had, in fact, been acting since he was 14, ever since he did a fistful of commercials and educational outings before he moved into what Johnny would identify as television hell by playing the homeless Luke in *Growing Pains*. Soon after, he crossed over to movies, and although still some years away from establishing himself in the heart-throb stakes for the 1996 version of William Shakespeare's *Romeo & Juliet*, and two years later in James Cameron's *Titanic*, his performance opposite Robert De Niro in *This Boy's Life*, the same year he made *Gilbert Grape*, established him as the promising youngster he turned out to be.

In fact, DiCaprio was so brilliant in *Gilbert Grape* that he was suddenly in danger of being typecast, not merely as a troubled teenager, but as a *very* troubled teenager. It was even confirmed by the additional acclaim of his peers — a nomination for Best Supporting Actor at the 1994 Academy Awards.

But it didn't happen by accident. As DiCaprio himself explains, 'It was one of the hardest things I've ever done. I had to really research and get into the mind of somebody with a disability like that. I spent a few days at a home for mentally retarded teens. We just talked and I watched their mannerisms. People have these expectations that mentally retarded children are really crazy, but it's not so. It's refreshing to see them, because everything is new to them. They are completely spontaneous and focus on what is directly in their vision, what they experience at the moment. Playing Arnie was fun because everything I did was spontaneous.'

Hallstrom, too, noticed the focus. There was one particular autistic boy, he remembers, who very much became DiCaprio's role model. 'I took a lot of his mannerisms and made them my own,' confirmed the actor. 'I developed the character even more by adding the mannerisms of some of the other people I had met.'

Executive Producer, Alan C Blomquist couldn't agree more. 'Leonardo gives Arnie this child-like quality, playing him as very free and open and honest. He's a great counterpart to Johnny's Gilbert, who is so solemn and serious about life.' Some even thought that DiCaprio stole all Johnny's scenes, and everybody else's.

All the same, Johnny and DiCaprio were a marvellous combination. On location in Austin, Texas, DiCaprio recalls their brotherly relationship on and off camera. It was, he said, important 'to be just buddy-buddy with each other. Brothers don't necessarily have to say anything to each other. They can just sit in a room and be together and just be completely comfortable with each other.'

In many ways, Johnny was extremely like Gilbert, continues DiCaprio. 'But it wasn't something Johnny was trying to do. It naturally came out of him. I never quite understood what he was going through, because it wasn't some big emotional drama that was happening on the set every day, but subtle things I'd see in him. There's an element of Johnny that is extremely nice and extremely cool, but at the same time he's hard to figure out. But that makes him interesting.'

One of those things, elaborates DiCaprio, was when Johnny 'loved to see my facial expressions when I was disgusted by the smell of something gross, like decaying honeycomb, rotten eggs and pickled sausage. He'd give it to me to smell and I would do this gagging thing. In the end I couldn't stand it and charged him for the pleasure. I made about $500 dollars!'

Johnny, though, had once been on the receiving end himself. It happened when he inhaled the scent of a television remote control that had found its way into the anatomy of a girlfriend of Gibby Haynes, his friend and subsequent guitar player for Johnny's band. 'The look on his face was priceless,' Haynes laughs. But then again, Johnny openly admits he was 'an equal opportunities sniffer'.

Slowly, the rest of the cast took shape around the core of Johnny and DiCaprio. Juliette Lewis, best known at the time for her role in Woody Allen's *Husbands and Wives* would portray Johnny's love interest. But unlike Johnny and DiCaprio, she chose to remain aloof during filming. Even when she had the scenes with Johnny, it was no different. 'We never even talked to each other really. I worked with him, but I don't have a clue who he is as a person. When I'm at work, I just sort of go. My purpose is to do the job as well as possible and not go dancing and do all that other bullshit.'

And that, for now, meant concentrating on playing Becky, the caravanning tourist who gets stranded in Endora long enough to fall for Gilbert. 'I wanted to play her real still. Didn't want to fiddle and do a bunch of facial gestures or go crazy with her because she's sort of the same element in the movie. So I made a decision to be still and logical. My mind works like a computer. I can read scenes, and I'll know exactly how to behave. It just happens automatically. I don't have to do a lot of outside stuff to figure it out.'

Neither did Darlene Gates, albeit for different reasons. She actually did weigh 600lb, and came to the part almost by accident. She had been spotted by Hedges on a chat show about obesity and the problems associated with it, and although not a professional actress, she was the perfect choice. Not merely for her size, but also for the understanding she would have for the character.

At that point, conceded Gates, 'I hadn't left my house in five years, so I started taking correspondence courses to get my high school diploma. Then I found I was going to be a grandmother for the first time, and I wanted to be in the delivery room. It just seemed like I needed to do that, and so I went and did the talk show. I thought I was only one of a very small number, but there are many people like me out there.'

The hardest thing for her was the scene where Gilbert's mother leaves the family home for the first time in seven years and is driven by Gilbert to the police headquarters to fetch Arnie from the cell he has now been thrown into. His recent climbing escapades have left both police and emergency services alike in a quandary as to what to do with him for his own safety, so for the time being, they lock him up. Gilbert's mother is outraged, and storms into the police station to demand that her boy is released right there and then. No one, of course, argues. Not even Gerry, the duty sergeant. With Arnie back in the safe hands, the family leave as they arrived — together, amidst a crowd of onlookers who stop dead in their tracks to stare at the spectacle.

That scene, shudders Gates, 'was so real for me. I had to take time out afterwards because I burst into tears. But then so much of the film was real to me. An integral part of the story is letting people see how much bigotry and cruelty big people go through. I hope we set a trend. I hope it helped change people's attitudes and made them more tolerant.'

Certainly, that is what she hoped for. 'I think she shares what many overweight people do — a feeling that we are unacceptable. I'm glad to say that I don't feel that way any more. I found out that I do have something to offer, just like everyone else. The trick, I think, is just being patient until God reveals to you just what that something is.'

As far as the critics were concerned, it was one quirky role too many for Johnny. Richard Corliss writing in *Entertainment Weekly* was far more complimentary than most. 'DiCaprio and Gates bring loopy authenticity to their roles, and Depp is, as always, a most effacing star. Here, as in *Edward Scissorhands* and *Benny and Joon*, he behaves wonderfully on screen.'

But not everyone thought so. Quentin Curtis in his review of the film for the *Independent on Sunday* said it was a 're-run of his wistful comedy *Benny and Joon*, down to the nowheresville setting and the loopy kid he looks after'. The *Sunday Times* critic Anne Bilson went further when she observed that Johnny, 'might have been the next Tom Cruise except that his career choices are so wilfully non-commercial'. *Sky* magazine added: 'Depp's avoided one kind of stereotyping, but he faces the opposite danger; will he still be playing kooks when he's 40?'

But Johnny was not concerned. 'I've been real lucky. People have mentioned that I like doing offbeat roles, but I've been lucky in the sense that I haven't been typecast. It's important to keep changing. There's a lot of stuff that I just don't buy into, like being an actor who takes himself so seriously that he pretends to be this tortured artist. I think that everybody has pain and an actor doesn't necessarily have more of it than others.'

Besides, he didn't need that sort of hell and he was damned if he was going to let it need him. But what he didn't know at the time was that he was about to underestimate the strength of his own emotions. Probably more than he thought possible.

CHAPTER 8

'Since I was a teenager I've been afraid of being a loser, a guy with no talent or ambition. No matter how much money I've made as an actor, I can't seem to get rid of this image of myself as a white trash loser.'

A Nightmare
On Sunset Boulevard

There are times in everybody's life when, suddenly and inexplicably, everything seems to go wrong. As Hallowe'en night 1993 neared, Johnny was closer to that state than he had ever felt before when one of Hollywood's most promising new young stars died of a drug overdose outside his club, The Viper Room.

In little more than 12 years, River Phoenix had established himself among the most significant actors of his generation and the least likely to hit the A-list of premature departures. In fact, his unique childhood raised by unconventional parents did everything to suggest the opposite. Time and again, his often bold decisions to speak out about the dangers of hard drugs and of his attitudes toward them did nothing but affirm his general aversion to recreational drugs of any sort. It was what won him the respect and admiration of fans around the world as he was propelled from teen star to cultural icon.

All the same, he spent as little time as he could in Hollywood. As much as his friends Keanu Reeves and Winona Ryder did their best to retreat from the hype of tinsel town, so did Phoenix. He simply deplored what he called its 'bad influences and superficial values'.

Indeed, both fans and the Hollywood insiders themselves have since struggled to make sense of the actor's death. Even a casual observer of tabloid headlines would not have put Phoenix down as the one likely to run into trouble.

It simply beggared belief that the child of hippie parents — someone with such Utopian ideals, who refused meat, dairy and fish products, campaigned for environmental issues such as saving the rainforests and the humane treatment of animals, refused to wear leather, and characteristically chose to hide away from the celebrity spotlight — could have died of a drug overdose. It just wasn't possible.

Situated on the corner of Larabee Street and Sunset Boulevard, Johnny's club was co-owned with rock star Chuck E Weiss, and had been ever since it opened in late summer 1993. The two had refurbished the little place into what was, for Johnny, a characteristically 1920s speakeasy around which the rest of the décor would subsequently revolve. Even the cigarette girls Johnny hired were throwbacks to the period.

As much, in fact, as the tiny centrepiece dance floor that was surrounded by five equally tiny booths. One was

seemingly permanently reserved for Johnny's agent Tracey
Jacobs, adorned with a 'Don't Fuck With It' gold plaque. The
corner stage would accommodate Johnny, his friends and
musicians for the informal jamming sessions that often took
place. Several, Johnny recalls, with Phoenix's band, Aleka's
Attic, who were all set to play on the evening Phoenix died
from the same lethal drug combination that killed John
Belushi 11 years earlier.

For Phoenix, it was an evening that had started out
much earlier that Saturday night at his suite in The Nikko
Hotel, west of Los Angeles. Even room service noted how
chaotic it was — loud music, and a highly intoxicated-looking
Phoenix, which could probably be attributed to drugs and
alcohol.

But Phoenix wasn't concerned. Nor apparently was
his party; Sammantha Mathis, his girlfriend at the time and
co-star of his then latest movie *The Thing Called Love*; his
brother Leaf, sister Rain and Red Hot Chilli Pepper
guitarist Flea. What Phoenix must have wondered, however,
was how on earth he was going to make it through the
evening, even as he made his way across town slumped in
the back of his car.

It hit him almost as soon as he arrived at The Viper
Room. Barely able to stand, concedes one waitress, 'he kept
leaping up and bumping into things. His words were so
slurred you could barely understand him.' But still the drinks
kept coming.

Although unclear as to exactly what happened next,
some suggested the actor moved into a backroom behind
the corner stage to consume what is called a 'speedball', a
lethal cocktail of drugs. Then he returned to his table, and

without warning, he started vomiting. That was when some of his party took him to the bathroom to clean him up. There they splashed cold water on his face in their attempts to stop the actor trembling. But, sadly, to no avail. By the time they returned to their table it was clear he was well on the way to becoming an overdose victim. 'He just looked completely stoned,' observed one guest that evening. 'It was quite apparent that he was on something. He was table-hopping and bumping into tables.'

Not only that, but he was having seizures, falling down hard on to the table and sliding away beneath it. Even more frightening was the difficulty he had breathing. Even as he passed Johnny playing on stage on his way outside to grab some fresh air with Sammantha, Leaf and Rain, it was no better. In fact, he was now only minutes away from losing his life. He collapsed on to the pavement in a fit of violent twitching and thrashing. According to one photographer outside the club, he looked 'like a fish out of water, flapping around the sidewalk like a guppy'.

The strange thing, he continues, was that 'people walked by, no crowd formed and no one stopped to help'. It was, after all, Hallowe'en when every oddball in the area was on parade either dressed as victims of drive-by killings, or bloody surfers cut in two by their surfboards. The only difference was that the scene on the pavement in front of The Viper Room was real, even if the passers-by did shrug it off as just another part of the freak show.

From that moment, Leaf panicked, rushed into The Viper Room foyer, picked up the phone and dialled 911, begging the emergency services to hurry. The same message was later played repeatedly on radio and television in the aftermath of the tragedy. 'My brother's having seizures,' Leaf sobbed. 'I'm thinking he had Valium or something. You must get here. Please, because he's dying.' But, sadly, it was too late. By the time the medics arrived, just minutes later, River Phoenix was pronounced to be in full fatal cardiac arrest. It was nine minutes before two o'clock on Hallowe'en morning, just three hours after he had arrived at Johnny's club.

'There hasn't been anything this catastrophic and dramatic,' declared *Variety* columnist Amy Archerd, 'since James Dean and Natalie Wood died.' It was endorsed by the tributes that swiftly accumulated outside The Viper Room. 'The Eternal River Flows' read an inscription on a watercolour etching at the pavement altar festooned with incense candles. 'A true individual who will be remembered,' said a note as a teenager stared quietly while others wept. 'It's too sad,' sobbed a man from Glasgow standing next to four girls in baseball caps. 'He was no age at all, was he?'

'He had this ability to observe everything going on around him without really being part of it,' said another. 'He seemed able to separate himself from his surroundings.' But not everyone was sympathetic. Rush Limbaugh, the right-wing television and radio chat show host, certainly wasn't. She even condemned the media's attention to it.

'From the moment his death was discovered, you would have thought the President of the United States had been assassinated here ... that we've lost some great contributor to the social and human condition. This guy, look at his name! River Phoenix! He's the son of a couple of whacked-out hippies.'

Johnny was astounded, and a lot of other people shared his indignation. It was probably one of the reasons he couldn't bring himself to talk about the incident. Well, not immediately anyway. 'The thing is, he came with his guitar to the club. What a beautiful thing that he shows up with his girl on one arm and his guitar on the other. He came to play and he didn't think he was going to die — nobody thinks they're gonna die. He wanted to have a good time. It's dangerous, but that's the thing that breaks my heart — first he died, but also that he showed up with his guitar. That's not an unhappy kid.'

Neither did he see Phoenix's use of drugs as anything more than a dreadful mistake, one he himself could understand. 'He was a great actor and a great young man, a great human being. He had a great family, a very level view of life and a promising future. This is my quarrel with the press — they could have said, "Look, this was a normal guy, who had some things he was confused about, and he made a mistake. Anybody could make that same fatal mistake, and it could be any one of us. Watch yourself!" But nobody said that.'

Even sicker than the media's attempts to snare Johnny, however, were the allegations against him of contributing to Phoenix's death by running a club like The Viper Room in the first place. And, secondly, by allowing back-room drug abuse, which, the papers suggested, Johnny knew all about. Not surprisingly, he was adamant. 'There was a lot of speculation going on,' he retorted.

'A lot of people were playing backyard detective and exploiting the situation to get ratings and to sell newspapers and magazines. The tabloids were complete fiction. It's really tragic and sad. How many times did we need to hear that 911 tape? How many times did they have to print that stuff? For how long does Leaf have to live with the rewinding in his head? We've become a society of ambulance chasers.

Everybody focused on the bad, nobody's interested in the good ... I've worked in this business for ten years, and to say I opened a nightclub to allow people to do drugs, even in the bathroom — do people think I'm insane? Do they think I'm going to throw eveything away — even my own children's future, so people could get high in a nightclub? It's ridiculous.'

Once again, Johnny asserted, 'the press was trying to tarnish his memory in the minds of all those people who loved him. What it all boils down to is a very sweet guy who made one big, fatal mistake. It's a mistake we're all capable of. What took place was so heavy that I didn't even retaliate against the accusations towards me. The fact is, I was there that night. It was my club. I said, "I refuse to be a part of this morbid circus that you fucking ambulance chasers have going. Fuck off!"'

Even Sal Jenco, Johnny's childhood friend from Florida, now running The Viper Room for him, had to put up with another scandal when former television soap star and now established singer, Jason Donovan, collapsed, less fatefully, of course, outside the club, ironically echoing the River Phoenix tragedy. The difference was that Donovan survived.

He would not, however, be so concerned with the tabloid onslaught that followed. Britain's *News of the World*, for instance, went as far to call Johnny's club DEPP'S DEN OF SEX, DRUGS AND DEATH.

In a weekend so dominated by such wild accusations, the stories fell horribly flat. After all, Johnny had never said, 'I run a place that is filled with drugs and people screwing on the tables.' He defended The Viper Room by saying, 'This is a nightclub — it's a decent place. The Mayor of West Hollywood is having her reception here, for Christ's sake, why don't they write about that? Because it doesn't sell magazines unless they get a photograph of the Mayor with a syringe stuck in the back of her neck ...'

Johnny was less reticent, of course, on The Viper Room's notoriety. 'It became a scene instantly when we opened it. I never had any idea that it was going to do that. I really thought it was gonna just be this cool little underground place. You can't even see the place. There's no sign on Sunset. It's just a black building and the only sign is on Larabee, a tiny little sign, real subtle, and I figured it would be low key.

'What soured me was what happened after all that took place on Hallowe'en, the unfortunate passing of River. I closed it down for two weeks out of respect, so the kids could write their messages and leave flowers. I thought that was real sweet of them. I knew for the next month or so it was just gonna be a gawk feast, just filled with gawkers and tourists, Grave-line Tours, all that shit. I just didn't go around for a while. We've weeded out the gawkers, now it's back to being a good place.'

Johnny was also back to being in a good place. Indeed, it was February 1994, four months after River Phoenix's death, when a friend introduced him to Kate Moss, the waif model from Calvin Klein's Obsession fragrance and Yves Saint Laurent ads.

She was visiting New York and had stopped off at Manhattan's Café Tebac. Johnny, too, was in town where he would also have coffee at the same bistro. 'It wasn't all that romantic,' remembers Johnny. 'She was sitting at a table with some friends, and I knew one of them.' He invited them over. 'And that's how we met and we haven't been apart since. We're just having fun. A lot of fun. She's a real down-to-earth English girl who gives me no chance to get big-headed about my life.'

Kate Moss and Johnny Depp — it was another relationship made in tabloid heaven. As much, or perhaps even more, than Johnny and Winona. Even though Kate wasn't an actress and didn't have the whole world in love with her, she had nonetheless firmly established herself among the supermodels of her generation — Claudia Schiffer, Cindy Crawford and Naomi Campbell were the others.

Born in Addiscombe, Surrey, on 16 January 1974, when Johnny was 11, and raised in Croydon, another London suburb, Kate was spotted in between flights at New York's John F Kennedy Airport by Storm Model Agency boss Sara Doukas. She immediately decided that she wanted to represent her. Even if Kate was shocked by this sudden turn of events, she was also excited. 'I'd seen her judging a *Clothes Show* competition so I knew she was for real.' She was just 14 at the time.

Even if Kate's fame was not exactly handed to her on a plate, it was at least delivered to her door. Two years after she met Doukas, the same year Johnny met Winona, the agent came up trumps. That summer, British magazine *The Face* was looking for a girl to define the waif look for the cover of their next issue. If there was one thing Kate definintely was, she was waifish. And waifish still remains the word that best describes her.

In fact, some even suggested that the picture — shot by Corrine Day — of Kate's skeletal frame went a long way to encouraging *anorexia nervosa* and other eating disorders in young teenage girls who would try to emulate her. In fact, it was now a red-hot favourite for debate.

Kate was suddenly everywhere. Magazines, catwalks, billboards. Even aeroplanes. Quite an accomplishment for a model whose CV now includes such culture-defining names as Chanel and Gianni Versace. Kate remembers, 'Corrine phoned me the other day and said "You know, you don't know how famous you are. You're topless on every other bus."' Kate was still down-to-earth enough to be astonished.

Kate, of course, wished the tabloid press had been less attentive to the critical comments that followed. How many times would she have to defend her appearance? How many times would she have to explain that she had an exceptionally fast metabolism? It irritated her even more the day she was tagged 'Superwaif'. Finally, losing patience she snapped, 'All those anorexic things do bother me. I know I'm going to be called a waif for ever. And I hate it.'

Far more damaging, of course, was everything else the gossip columnists blamed her for, everything from elder women's self-hatred, the rise in child abuse, the fall in the exchange rate, global warming, football hooliganism ...

In the years to come, of course, Johnny would also snap at the constant swiping at Kate's ultra-slim appearance. 'She eats like a champ,' he reflected years later. 'She really puts it away. Why punish somebody because they have a good metabolism? Because they digest their food better? It doesn't make any sense.'

Kate agreed. 'I am just on my way out to dinner,' she wrote years later in the introduction to her book of photographs, 'to eat a massive steak, loads of very fattening potatoes with lots of butter.' Not that it would make much difference as far as the press were concerned. 'You'd like to believe her,' wrote one of those critics, 'but you can't imagine how she'd fit it all in. Even if her legs are hollow, there wouldn't be room for much more than a chip.'

But maybe that was something to do with the pictures that adorned the pages of her lavish coffee table hardback. Everything from Kate lolloping down a Mexican beach to shadow-boxing in New York. Looking very 1970s, looking scary, looking wise, innocent, carefree, hunted, glamorous, gorgeous, asleep. Kate close up, Kate far away. In knickers, in feathers, in need of a wash.

Perhaps it is because her rise to megastardom was so straightforward that Kate has not lost the qualities that so entranced the fashion-spotters who first saw her. 'What Kate Moss has is a brilliant and quite unerring fashion instinct,' wrote the fashion critic in Britain's *Guardian*.

'She's fantastic at interpreting photographers' ideas, an exceptional trendsetter, a great artist-as-model. When you flick through her book, one is struck by her versatility, her never-ending, ever-changing ability to put over clothes. It's an odd talent.'

Two years before that high praise, of course, was the offer that would elevate Kate out of simple modelling assignments to establish her as a genuine supermodel. Calvin Klein wanted her to appear topless alongside Marky Mark in their latest advertising campaign. Kate accepted.

But again, there was a sting in the tail. And this time it wasn't simply the critical objections to her appearance that tormented her. Kate also found herself the victim of the gossip factory. It was what she attributes to the breakdown of her failed relationship with photographer Mario Sorrenti several months before she met Johnny.

Even then, when the couple went public with their relationship, the tabloids hounded them. Johnny, though, was unconcerned. At that point, he said, 'the press said so many shitty things that I couldn't give a fuck any more. As long as they're not hurting my family or someone I love, they can say I have a fetish for midget amputees for all I care.'

Deep inside, however, that was his only defence. 'I don't talk about it and she doesn't talk about it, because it's nobody's business,' he insisted. 'This is a rumour-filled society and if people want to sit around and talk about whom I've dated, then I'd say they have a lot of spare time and should consider other topics. Or masturbation.'

As Johnny had already pointed out, Kate did her best to shrug off the attention. But she also acknowledged there was no way to avoid enthusing about her new found love. Not even to the *Daily Mail*. In echoes of Johnny and Winona, she raved, 'I can't believe it. It's like nothing that has ever happened to me before. I knew straight away, knew that it was different. I just never felt anything like this before. I knew, this was it.' Not only that, she continues, but 'I fancied him before I met him!'

Once again, the gossip columnists couldn't go wrong. And, of course, the age gap between Johnny and Kate was their number one concern, much as it had been over Johnny and Winona. Although this time, the gap was even greater.

Even though the couple initially focused on the juvenile side of their relationship, the ubiquitous Hollywood insiders found their mutual passion for funfair rides a far cry from the fascination for Beat poetry and literature Johnny had shared with Winona. 'We love going to Magic Mountain,' confessed Johnny, 'and doing all the fastest rides, but you have to go first thing in the morning, or you just end up spending all day signing autographs.'

'I knew from the first moment we talked that we were going to be together,' admitted Kate later. The first few months of the couple's life was indeed spent together. Even when she turned 21, Johnny threw a surprise birthday party at The Viper Room, where he covered the club in fresh roses and balloons. Gloria Gaynor sang 'I Will Survive'. An Elvis impersonator joined Thelma Houston in another singalong, and Johnny played on stage with INXS vocalist Michael Hutchence.

But the first time out in public was at the Los Angeles night spot Smashbox where Johnny would launch his film short on the dangers of drug addiction during a *Vogue* benefit to aid the Drug Abuse Resistance Education programme before an audience of 800.

Banter followed in the form of the public information promo shorts Johnny had made from his *21 Jump Street* days, and the 15-minute question and answer AIDS documentary he appeared in with Winona being made at the time for her mother's production video company.

Now, he had the opportunity to turn his own personal experiences into a plea for youngsters to avoid drugs at all costs. According to *Esquire*, the film was 'a gruesome but provocative excursion into the world of hard drugs'. It also questioned Johnny's own reported drug use. With the River Phoenix tragedy continuing to prey on his mind, perhaps nobody realised just how much it had affected Johnny until he spoke out.

'It's all in the past,' he swore. 'I've been taunted by

the press and put in a position of having to defend myself. I've done nothing wrong. I've even made an anti-drug movie, and I hope kids learn a lot from it, that drugs are no escape. There are other ways of escaping, like books, painting and writing.'

Only a few weeks after the Smashbox gig, Johnny and Kate were spotted again, this time vacationing on St Barts. On another occasion, while Johnny was writing *The Brave*, they were seen in Mustique with Noel Gallagher and his then girlfriend, later wife, Meg Matthews. Long before that, of course, the couple were spotted at Manhattan's Fez Club for a Johnny Cash concert. And less than a day after he finished filming *Don Juan DeMarco*, Johnny caught a flight to Paris and made his way to Kate's catwalk and couture shows where she gave him a ring-shaped platinum rattle filled with black pearls. And for Kate, a strand of diamonds. They couldn't, insisted one observer, keep their hands, lips, mouths and legs off each other.

Maybe that was true. But he also confessed that a persistent favourite was feet. Or at least, that's what he told *FHM* magazine. 'They are very, very important,' he insisted. 'They are way up there on the priority list. About top two. A bad pair of feet, let's see, would be with long toenails. I can remember seeing my great grandmother's toenails. She was a full-blooded Cherokee. Her toenails were really long and curled like cashews. Long toenails are a bad move. Horrible, can't even think about it. Just an awful image. Feet say a lot. If a girl doesn't take care of her feet there may be problems elsewhere.'

Good feet or not, 'she must be great,' said Sarah Jessica Parker, Johnny's co-star from *Ed Wood*, in her praise for Kate. 'I'm going to assume that and endow her with good qualities because I can't imagine Johnny spending time with anyone who wasn't his equal.'

'He is incorruptible,' agreed Faye Dunaway, his leading lady from *Arizona Dream*. 'He always believes in this pure way about love. He's got those kinds of values and it's instinctive with him. This isn't something he's worked out in his head. I love that he believes in love.'

But not everyone agreed. Tally Chanel, the B-movie actress whom Johnny had met in July 1990, was far more negative in her perception of Kate, inviting her not to put up with the actor's temper tantrums. 'Johnny needs an accomplice to end up in trouble, and it's obvious Kate has a lot to do with his recent behaviour.'

One of those occasions came seven months after Johnny and Kate had met, and was at the Mark Hotel in New York City. 'Let's say my stay wasn't particularly comfortable,' was the way Johnny explained it after attending some *Ed Wood* press conferences he was in town for.

The difficulties seemed to start from the moment he checked in. He had already been put out because of not being able to book into his regular haunt The Carlyle. It wasn't the fact that the Mark's Presidential Suite wasn't up to scratch. Far from it. As far as Johnny was concerned, it was the night security guard Jim Keegan who ranked highly among his problems. It was an instinct that would later prove to be the correct one.

'It seemed like the guy couldn't stand Johnny,' recalls Jonathan Shaw, his friend and tattooist. It probably didn't help that 'Johnny was dressed in leather and jeans, not at all fancy like everybody else in the joint.' Johnny couldn't agree more. 'The guy was a little froggy and he decided he was going to "get in the famous guy's face". I don't really take too well to that.'

Kate was also in town and stayed with Johnny in the hotel from that first Monday through to the early hours of Tuesday. In fact, it was early that morning, just before dawn, something happened that would alter the course of Johnny's public profile — and image — for ever.

Occupying the suite next to Johnny and Kate was Roger Daltry, lead singer of the Sixties rock group The Who, and in his time was probably as famous for his hotel trashing as for his band's musical focus. But that didn't stop him calling the front desk to complain about a disturbance next door. The only difference, explained Johnny later, is that The Who would have done a better job, 'and then been applauded for it. I was arrested and incarcerated. Age is a wonderful thing, isn't it? Keith Moon would have been very embarrassed for him ... But he was probably used to being embarrassed for him.'

All the same, the complaint was enough to send Keegan rushing to investigate. The security guard was, according to Johnny, fired up from the start of their confrontation. He had, since Johnny's arrival, monitored his every move in and out of the hotel. 'The guy probably had too many cups of coffee that night,' laughs Johnny at the memory. 'He was particularly feisty, and he decided to call the shots in a way that I didn't think was particularly necessary.'

Johnny explains, 'If I walk into an antique shop and I bend down and look at something over here and I accidentally knock a pot off the rack, it's $3,000, of course, I'd pay for it. If I bust a piece of glass, I smash a mirror or whatever, I'll pay for it. I can probably handle the bill. That's it.'

But it wasn't it as far as Keegan was concerned. He took exception to whatever had gone on in the Presidential Suite and instructed him to leave the room — and the hotel — there and then. If not, he would call the police. Johnny apologetically offered to pay for any damage he had caused, but certainly didn't feel it was necessary for him to check out. True to his word, Keegan called the New York Police Department and 30 minutes later, Johnny was escorted by three officers from the 19th Precinct — out of the hotel and in handcuffs.

For the next 48 hours, Johnny was detained in three different cells at Precinct House, at Central Booking, and in the 'tombs' behind New York Central Police Headquarters where he was apparently mobbed by a horde of female police officers. Apart from one. Officer Eileen Perez was seemingly unimpressed by Johnny's presence. 'I don't think she likes me,' he smiled. 'But I bet if she saw me in a mall, she'd ask for my autograph.'

That is probably true. But at the same time, in the official police report, Keegan listed ten damaged items: two damaged seventeenth century picture frames and prints; a china lamp stand; a Chinese pot; a shattered glass tabletop; broken coffee table legs; broken wooden shelves; a shattered vase; cigarette burns on the carpet; and a split red desk chair.

David Breitbart, Johnny's attorney and New York criminal lawyer, attached to the litigation, said, 'That crazy damage figure they asked for was also for what he owed for the room two nights before, three nights after, something like that.' Even Marlon Brando was concerned. According to Breitbart, 'he said he was very concerned about Johnny's well-being and if there was anything he could do to help, he would like to.' Interestingly enough, neither Keegan nor the hotel's general manager Raymond Bickson would discuss the incident. Not with the press anyway.

Although Johnny didn't dispute the incident, he did offer an explanation. 'It wasn't a great night for me. I'm not trying to excuse what I did or anything like that, because it's someone else's property and you got to respect that. But you get into a head space, and you're human.'

The press, of course, was another matter entirely. Pictures of Johnny's arrest that decorated the front pages did nothing more than reinforce his image as a hell-raising party monster. Once again, the gossip columnists couldn't go wrong. 'I was just stressed out,' was how Johnny would explain away his behaviour. 'I'm human and I get angry like everyone else. I get frustrated and I just lashed out. Big deal. We're talking about an actor who might have assaulted a piece of furniture. I found myself on the covers of all the newspapers, as if this incident was of more importance than the invasion of Haiti. Firstly, you should be allowed to be a human being. Secondly, you should be allowed to have emotion, and thirdly, you should be allowed to have a private life.' Apparently, a private life was out of the question.

Even Betty Sue, Johnny's mother, now married to her third husband, Robert Palmer, was in shock. All the same, she got over it, Johnny recalls. 'She didn't like seeing me in handcuffs on TV, but she knows I'm not a bad person.' Neither did she like the way Johnny was kitted out — especially the green knitted hat and the sunglasses. 'She thought she'd taught me how to dress better than that.' Not

Johnny's haunting good looks have indubitably helped to propel him from teen star to cultural icon. He is pictured here at the 1995 *Nick of Time* première.

Johnny with Winona Ryder, shown here at the 1991 Golden Globe awards. She was his highest profile girlfriend before Kate Moss. They were introduced by a friend in 1989.

After his relationship with Winona failed, Johnny was spotted frequently with Kate Moss. They are shown here in London.

Top: On holiday in Mustique with Kate, Noel Gallagher and his wife Meg, Johnny displays his dislike of the ever ravenous paparazzi.

Bottom left: Johnny during a book-reading in New York to promote *Fear and Loathing in Las Vegas*.

Bottom right: With Betty Sue, his mother. He had her name tattooed inside a large red heart on his left bicep.

Johnny had met Hunter S Thompson long before he was chosen to star in the adaptation of the brilliant road novel, Fear and Loathing in Las Vegas.

Posing for a London photocall before a rare appearance on *Top of the Pops* in September 1994. He played alongside The Pogues.

Inset: Vanessa Paradis met Johnny in July 1998; she captivated him with her natural charm, and he moved into her Paris home after just a few months.

On set for The Astronaut's Wife, for which Johnny was reputedly offered $8 million, possibly his highest earning role at that time.

Johnny must surely have relished the prospect of starring in the frenetic drug-crazed road movie *Fear and Loathing in Las Vegas*. He is shown here at the première.

that John Waters, Johnny's director from *Cry Baby*, would agree.

'He looked good under arrest. I loved the handcuffs — they always work. Criminal movie star is a really good look for Johnny. The success of hotel room trashing should be calculated by the amount of damage, divided by the amount of column inches.' Even more damaging, of course, was the ostracism that his teenage niece and nephew would have to put up with at high school. Friends and pupils alike would tell them, 'Your uncle Johnny is a fucking maniac.'

Even though, as Johnny himself would point out, 'they gotta live with that stuff, too,' there was no let-up in the aftermath of the Mark Hotel débâcle. If anything it got worse. Johnny's alleged past with drugs and alcohol was still news. Now more so than ever since he had joined the litany of celebrity hotel trashers first started when Beethoven slung a chair through the window of a Vienna hotel room.

Even Leonardo DiCaprio's cameo role as a teen idol rowing furiously with his girlfriend and trashing a hotel room in Woody Allen's 1998 ensemble piece *Celebrity* was considered by many a depiction of Johnny's own Mark Hotel incident.

True or not, Johnny said, 'Now they can say they have this little bit of history, this ridiculous morsel of history. They can say "We had Johnny Depp arrested". Hotels are my home. I live in hotels more than I live in my house. If it had been you, nothing would have happened. They would have come to the room and said, "What's going on?" You would have said, "I'll pay for the damages, and I'm terribly sorry."'

Overlooking the negative aspects of the incident,

Faye Dunaway agrees with that summation. 'Sometimes you feel like you've just to kick over the traces, and the Mark took advantage of it. A publicity trip; it's outrageous. I would probably have smashed up the lobby after that. I think they should count themselves luckly that he didn't.'

Johnny, on the other hand, would later find the whole thing preposterous. Not surprising really when you consider 'I had to go to jail for assaulting a picture frame and a lamp!' The papers' depiction of him drunk and having a huge fight with Kate, he said, was 'complete bullshit. But, you know, let's say the guy over here in the bar, he's having a hard day, and eventually — one more stabbing in the toe — the guy's got to hit something. So you punch a wall, or do this and that. Fuck it, I'm normal and I want to be normal. But somehow, I'm just not allowed to be. Why can't I be human? I have a lot of love inside me, and a lot of anger inside as well. If I love somebody, then I'm going to love them. If I'm angry and I've got to lash out or hit somebody, I'm going to do it and I don't care what the repercussions are.'

Of course, the Mark Hotel wasn't the only episode in which Johnny had fallen out with the authorities. In fact his past seemed littered with similar bewildering lapses of behaviour. But why, Johnny asked, 'should I be considered any different than Joe the garbageman or the guy selling doughnuts down the street? Why can't I be as human as anybody, as emotional as anybody?'

Because, he concludes, 'we live in such an ambulance-chasing society. Where there's this judgemental mentality of waiting to expose the dirt on everyone. You'll never see one of those tabloids say, "God, what a nice guy Johnny Depp is!" because people just aren't interested.'

Certainly, he has a point. He had, after all, been variously reported to have been caught hanging, in a dangerously drunken stupor, from the top of the five-storey Beverly Center parking garage in Los Angeles with Nicholas Cage; blowing gasoline on to open flames; and he'd even been spotted screaming at Kate in the dining room of New York's Royalton Hotel. And while filming *21 Jump Street* at the show's Vancouver location in 1989, Johnny had allegedly assaulted a security guard, although the charges were later dropped.

And so they should have been, Johnny asserts. He was visiting with some friends late one evening at a hotel where he had once stayed. Although known to the staff, the security guard was determined to keep him out.

'He had a boner for me,' Johnny recalls. 'He had a wild hair up his ass, and he got real mouthy about with me, saying, "I know who you are, but you can't come up here unless you are a guest." The mistake he eventually made was to put his hands on me. I pushed him back, and then we sort of wrestled around a bit, and I ended up spitting in his face.'

On another occasion in the same period, Johnny and Gibby Haynes spotted some guy's motorcycle in Sherilyn Fenn's driveway, kidnapped the helmet, painted it garish colours, including the visor, and returned it with a love note. Overall, though, it was nothing more than a bit of harmless fun.

It did, though, occasionally get a little out of hand. One night, Johnny remembers, after a drinking competition with Iggy Pop, he was sued for smashing the window of the Lone Star Roadhouse on New York's 52nd Street, that showered glass over the woman who sued him. And if that wasn't enough, he had also been charged that same year with jaywalking in Beverly Hills, and even got into a squabble with the cop writing out the ticket when he was asked to put his cigarette out. Johnny refused, so the cop held his wrist until the cigarette fell from his hand. He lit another. 'Next thing I know, him and his partner handcuffed me and put me in a cell for a few hours. I'm not scared by those people. They just make me angry. You get the feeling there's nothing you can do.' But there is, he believes, 'Don't take shit from them.' But then again, he adds, 'I've known some cops who've seen way too many episodes of *Starksy and Hutch*.'

On another occasion when Johnny was drinking at London's Globe underground club, photographer Jonathan Walpole, a direct descendant of Sir Robert Walpole, told the *Evening Standard* how, when he accidentally picked up Johnny's drink, 'he pulled both my ears very hard. I informed him that this was not the customary way of greeting people in England, then some ape leapt on my back, put his arm around my neck and tried to force my head to the floor.'

But according to *Icon* magazine, some years later, Johnny had pulled Walpole's ears 'for repeatedly asking Kate Moss's friend for a cigarette and then taking a sip of her drink'. Not for the first time, Johnny's actions, it seemed, continued to be misinterpreted. But according to one friend it's just 'Johnny being Johnny'.

All the same, such antics were not altogether to Johnny's benefit, as Nicholas Cage shuddered when another reputed Hollywood bad boy, Mickey Rourke, trashed his New York Plaza suite just two months after the Mark Hotel incident, 'What's he trying to be? Johnny Depp?'

Sarah Jessica Parker, Johnny's co-star from *Ed*

Wood, was far more complimentary. 'Johnny has a very wise spirit, and he pays no heed to things that don't matter. He is internal in a way that is reflective but not isolating. He's a gentle, lovely person. And when I think of those things that have been written in the papers about him, it's as if they're talking about a totally different person.'

From the nightmare of the Mark Hotel and the rumours which still haunted Hollywood about the River Phoenix tragedy, Johnny, according to some, was in danger of walking the same path of self-destruction.

Johnny, however, did not agree. 'There have been times when I wasn't in a good place at all, I couldn't get a grip on what was going on around me, and I'd just get tanked. That's all right for a little while, but when it becomes a way of life, it's not good. It's really bad. And you spend all this time trying to recreate that first high you got, like when you're 13 or 14 and you get drunk or smoke a joint, or have sex, and it's the greatest — it never comes back. You're never going to get that feeling again.'

The hardest thing was the years 'I spent getting loaded to escape. But I never escaped, not once. I've got my demons. Alcohol or drugs can unleash those demons, or open up the doors for those demons to fly around.'

For some time, the press would refer to Johnny's Mark Hotel fiasco as nothing more than that. Even when, months later, Johnny would provide journalists with some new variations of what happened inside the Presidential Suite, his own sense of humour and mischievousness came through for most of it.

According to the *Sunday Times*, he said, 'I was sitting on the couch in my hotel room when a really big dachshund jumped out of the closet. I felt it was my duty to retrieve this animal, so I chased it for 20 minutes, but it wouldn't co-operate. Finally, it dived out the window and there I was, stuck with all this evidence.'

In another interview with *Empire* magazine, the sequence of events was even wilder. 'I think it was an armadillo. It felt like it was an armadillo. It may have been an elephant.'

But whatever he said, Johnny received another setback when he recovered his belongings from the Mark Hotel and checked back into his regular haunt The Carlyle, now with vacancies, for the rest of his stay. What he didn't expect to find, however, was the Marlon Brando autobiography that he'd been reading to be defaced — according to Johnny, it was clearly by someone at the Mark Hotel.

'Fuck you Johnny Depp' was the first message he came across as he flicked through the 468-page book. There were, of course, other messages on other pages. 'You're an asshole' read one. 'I hate you' ranted another.

That was the end; the fiasco had gone too far. If Johnny was incensed, then it was understandable. Far more important, he decided, was the basic need to get through it all with a minimum of scars.

He even developed elaborate plans to retreat from the hype of it all to catch up playing with his band Pee, or just simply 'P'. Now the five of them — Shane McGowan, Gibby Haynes, Bill Carter, Sal Jenco and Johnny — planned to sign with EMI's Capitol Records in mid-1995, aiming to produce their first album for release exactly one year later. Even the advance information sounded promising.

'With titles such as 'Michael Stipe', 'White Man Sings the Blues' and Daniel Johnston's 'I Save Cigarette Butts', the record barrels down P's rock 'n' roll highway and the four lanes sound irreverent, brash, raw and tough. Between the tongue-in-cheek cover of Abba's 'Dancing Queen' and the defiant 'Oklahoma', Carter's musical proficiency and Haynes' screwball vision blend with Depp's liquid guitar and Jenco's kinetic drumming in a volatile brew.'

And contributing his own footnote to Britain's musical legacy two years later, his friend Noel Gallagher of Oasis invited him to play on their latest album, *Be Here Now*. Johnny's 'actually one of the best guitarists I've ever seen,' Gallagher raves to this day. 'That's why we got him to play the slide guitar solo on "Fade In–Out" because I couldn't play it. Afterwards, when we were rehearsing for the tour, it took me about six months to work it out to see what he was actually playing.'

If, above all else, playing with P and Oasis was to reinforce or maybe remind people of his musical inspirations, then his next two movie roles would simultaneously prove to be the most controversial and challenging he had yet accepted.

CHAPTER 9

'I've always been attracted to losers.
I've never played the Hollywood game
just for the sake of winning. I do what
I want and, if it works within my
career, great. If not, fuck it.
I won't be a slave to success.'

Risky Roles

It was no surprise that Johnny agreed to link up with Tim Burton again for his next movie project. Neither was it surprising that Burton was so keen to cast Johnny in the title role. As Burton himself explains, 'I feel close to Johnny because I think somewhere inside we respond to similar things, and this was a chance after working on *Edward Scissorhands* to be more open.'

Ed Wood, Burton's marvellous biopic of Edward J Wood Jr, the ever-optimistic Hollywood hack of the title, occasional transvestite, and dubbed the world's worst film director, could have been custom-written for Burton's peculiar sensibilities, and the title role seemed to have been created for Johnny himself. Denise Di Novi, Johnny's producer from *Edward Scissorhands*, agreed. 'Ed Wood was extremely handsome and lovable, as is Johnny. More importantly, Johnny is an actor who takes risks and gives unusual characters the special treatment and dignity they deserve.'

Before any work could commence, however, Columbia, who had the picture in development, put the project on ice when Burton insisted on total creative licence for his film — and he wanted to shoot in black and white. That was the last straw as far as the studio was concerned and, one month before shooting was scheduled to start, Warners, Paramount and Fox all clamoured to pick up the option to make the movie. Burton shrugged and simply defected across town to Disney who ended up with a movie made on a respectable budget of $18 million.

It wasn't the first time that Columbia had pulled out of a Burton project. Before *Ed Wood*, Burton was set to direct an adaptation of Valerie Martin's spellbinding novel *Mary Reilly* with his *Beetlejuice* and *Edward Scissorhands* favourite, and now Johnny's ex-fiancée, Winona Ryder in the title role. It was the marvellous retelling of Robert Louis Stevenson's classic *Dr Jekyll and Mr Hyde* told through the eyes of a servant girl in the doctor's household, but Columbia took both Burton and Winona off the project.

'What happened was the studio wanted to push it,' Burton remembered. 'Whereas before, I could take my time to decide about things, in Hollywood you get shoved into this whole commercial thing. They want the movie.' But the last straw came when the studio, exasperated by what they perceived as his lack of urgency, told him they had another five directors who were interested in the project, insinuating that if he didn't get started, one of the others would.

They probably just wanted to hurry him up, but they chased him off instead. The whole process, Burton growls, turned him off, and he let the studio know it. 'Well, if you've got five other people who want to do it, maybe you should have them do it.'

Looking back, Burton reasons, 'Basically, they speeded me out of the project because they saw it in a certain way,' and he saw it in another. But this wasn't his only reason for dropping the project he had been so keen to complete. 'They also saw it with Julia Roberts replacing Winona, and once Stephen Frears had taken over as director, that is what they got.

Burton and Winona took the disappointment stoically, although Burton did not have long to mourn. *Ed Wood* awaited him just around the corner. In fact, he had quickly become interested in the project when it was brought to his attention by Larry Karaszewski and Scott Alexander, screenwriters of the *Problem Child* movies. They had toyed with the idea of writing a film about Wood ever since they were room-mates at the University of Southern California film school. Irritated at being thought of as solely writers of kids' movies, they wrote a ten-page treatment and pitched the idea to *Heathers* director Michael Lehmann with whom they shared much of their time at the USC. He, in turn, took the project to his *Heathers* producer Denise Di Novi who immediately struck up a deal for Lehmann to direct, and herself to produce alongside Burton.

It was really when *Mary Reilly* fell through that Burton became more interested in directing *Ed Wood* himself, but only on the understanding it could be done quickly. With this in mind, Karaszewski and Alexander set about writing their screenplay, and delivered it to Burton six weeks later. He read the first draft and deemed it suitable enough to direct as it stood, without any changes or rewrites. That in itself was unusual.

Wood, the director of such cult classics as *Glen or Glenda*, *Bride of the Monster* and, most infamously, *Plan 9 from Outer Space*, died in 1978 aged 54, penniless and forgotten. Sadly, he achieved near legendary status only posthumously, in the early Eighties. Just as video recorders began to liberate viewers from the tyranny of television programming schedules, the films of Ed Wood captured cult followings as he all but took up permanent residence in Michael and Harry Medved's book of *The Golden Turkey Awards* in which he was granted the dubious honour of being the 'World's Worst Film Director'.

Born in Poughkeepsie, New York in 1924, Wood lived his entire life on the cusp of Hollywood, aspiring to be the next Orson Welles, but never even coming remotely close. A famed transvestite with a fondness for Angora sweaters and an engaging personality, Wood surrounded himself with a bizarre côterie of admirers and wannabes — his girlfriend Dolores Fuller, television horror hostess, Vampira (the stage name for Maila Nurmi), Swedish wrestler Tor Johnson and camp television psychic Criswell, all of whom believed Ed would one day make them stars.

In 1953, Wood met his idol Bela Lugosi, a Hungarian immigrant and the celebrated star of Universal's 1930 version of *Dracula*, but in the two decades that had passed since the release of the classic horror tale, Lugosi had slipped into virtual obscurity, had became addicted to morphine, and was by the time Wood found him, trying out coffins in a mortuary. Wood, however, was not discouraged, and vowed to revitalise Lugosi's career by casting him in his movies, and subsequently landed him with roles in *Glen or Glenda*, Wood's autobiographical tale of a transvestite, played by Wood himself under the name of Daniel Davis, and *Bride of the Monster*. Even the small amount of footage he shot of Lugosi leaving his home shortly before his death found its way into Wood's worst movie, *Plan 9 from Outer Space*, the one Wood was certain would establish his name. It did, but for all the wrong reasons.

Karaszewski and Alexander's script centred around Wood's life through the three movies, and focused on his relationship with Lugosi. Burton acknowledged that it was not unlike his own friendship with Vincent Price. 'There was an aspect of Wood's relationship with Bela Lugosi that I liked,' he explained. 'He befriended him at the end of his life, and without really knowing what that was like, I connected with it on the level that I did with Vincent Price, in terms of how I felt about him. Meeting Vincent had an incredible impact on me, the same impact Ed must have felt meeting and working with his idol.'

Burton's first choice of actor was, of course, Johnny, whom Burton called the minute he knew the project was on. As soon as he answered the phone, Johnny recalls, 'Tim asked me to meet him right away at the Formosa Café.' Twenty minutes later, they were talking about the project over some beer at the bar. And five minutes after that, Johnny continues, 'I was committed, completely committed. I was already familiar with Wood's films, and I knew that nobody could tell his story better than Tim. Tim's passion became my passion. I've turned parts down and regretted them in the future, and I think I would have been as sick as a dog if I had walked away from this one.'

All the same, it was not an easy role for Johnny to prepare for. In fact, he would most probably say it was one of the most difficult he had taken on. Never before had he played a real-life person, and he knew it would be very different from his past portrayals of fictional characters. 'I think it would be foolish for any film-maker to say they could hit the nail right on the head when trying to capture someone's life,' explained Johnny. Right from the start, 'Tim and the writers wanted to make something that captured a real Hollywood icon, and I think we did that. It isn't really about exploitation. This is a homage. A real, weird homage, but nevertheless, a respectable one.'

Equally difficult was the lack of visual material available for Johnny to tackle. Aside from Wood's own film appearance in *Glen or Glenda*, some rare silent behind-the-scenes footage, and a few black-and-white stills, there was little else. Not for the first time, Johnny would have to rely upon his own instincts, and indeed, his own perceptions of what he considered Wood to be like in reality. But that didn't stop him leaping into the role without hesitation.

'I read whatever I could get my hands on,' Johnny continued to explain. 'It was completely accepted that the details of Wood's life were a little muddled. Tim wanted to capture the spirit of the guy, and I had to exhibit that. I watched the films, and then put different people together in my brain. I wanted to make him extremely optimistic, innocent and a brilliant showman all at the same time. He was a man who loved making films.' It was, Johnny elaborated, 'his whole life and he didn't allow anything to discourage him'. Neither did Johnny. In fact, his performance as Ed Wood is a role which many people still consider Johnny's broadest and most theatrical.

Slowly, the rest of the cast took shape around the core of Johnny. Martin Landau was recruited to play Bela Lugosi; Bill Murray became Wood's transvestite friend Bunny Breckinridge; Jeffrey Jones, from Burton's own *Beetlejuice*, was chosen for the role of Criswell; Lisa Marie, a former model and now Burton's girlfriend, would play Vampira; real-life wrestler George 'The Animal' Steele became his Swedish counterpart Tor Johnson; Sarah Jessica Parker played Wood's girfriend Dolores; and Patricia Arquette was cast as Ed's wife Kathy. Once again, Burton proved his casting choices to be another excellent mix of talent.

That is certainly what he strived for. Aside from Johnny, 'I wanted to go with some knowns and unknowns,' Burton confirmed. 'It was like trying to get a mix of people, just like in Ed Wood's movies. I wanted it to have its own kind of weird energy,' just as *Beetlejuice* and *Edward Scissorhands* before had done. As far as Burton was concerned, weird was good, weird was acceptable, and weird was successful. One of his strongest beliefs — that Hollywood conventions are simply there to be broken and that an audience will happily watch you break them as long as they are entertained — from that point of view, *Ed Wood* would be no different.

Outside his own circle of colleagues, Johnny was considered an odd choice for the part. In fact, rumours circulated around Hollywood that he had already taken his research for the role far beyond what was expected. But according to Scott Alexander, he was only wearing woman's underwear and Angora sweaters as part of his everyday routine to prepare for the role. He even told Alexander how he would grab the little hairs over his nipples and just try to twist them around, absent-mindedly, while he was pacing around.

If Burton was concerned, it was only the fact that 'Ed would have to be in drag through portions of the film, and people in drag are real easy targets, but Johnny was so credible that he pulls it off without making it laughable. Besides, he really looks great in those clothes.'

There had, of course, been others before him who had appeared in drag. Most notably Robin Williams as Mrs Doubtfire and Dustin Hoffman in 1982's *Tootsie*. The only difference was that both were already middle-aged by the time they made those movies, and would most probably be far less concerned about the consequences of dressing up in women's clothing. But Johnny needn't have worried. If anything, his performance, whether in or out of drag, delighted both audiences and critics alike on the film's release.

Not even Landau was concerned. 'When I played a homosexual in Hitchcock's *North by Northwest*, I was asked if I was concerned that people would think I was gay. "Of course not," I said. It's like with Johnny — if you're comfortable with yourself, you're comfortable with yourself. Otherwise, you shouldn't be an actor.'

Not only that, but before filming got under way, Johnny recalls, 'I got a package from Miss Vera's Finishing School in New York City. They teach men to become transvestites, how to behave like women. It was a bunch of stuff, literature and photographs. The letter said, "We heard you were doing this film. We could help you become a woman." I pondered the thought of going there to investigate what they were doing.'

According to costume designer Colette Atwood, that wasn't really necessary at all. Although it would prove challenging to transform one of Hollywood's hottest young actors into an actress, she knew exactly how to do it. 'When Ed is dressed as a man, he's a basic guy with shirt, dark slacks, tie, vest. That way, when he's in drag, it's a very big shock, and the distinction is clear cut. When he's a woman, we pad out his hips and give him a bust and stuff. Actually, Johnny looks great as a woman. The first time we put him in Angora we were saying "God, he looks beautiful."'

Johnny, however, was not convinced, and he commented on how strange it was to play someone who had dressed in women's clothing. 'When I first looked in the mirror,' he confessed, 'I thought I was the ugliest woman I had ever seen. I mean, I looked huge in those clothes. Enormous!' The comfort, however, was unexpected. It even led him to understand the character he was playing. 'It was spookily comfortable. The only time I felt weird was when I had to do a striptease. But I didn't have any fear about what the audience might think. It would have spoiled the effect if I had looked uneasy in any way. However, I am getting better at walking in high heels.

'I've got some nice slips and hosiery and garters, a couple of nice brassières,' he continued. 'And I love Angora sweaters. Oh man, they're unbelievable. They feel really good. This girl I dated when I was a teenager, she had an

Angora sweater. When we broke up, I was upset, but not about her. It was the sweater.'

All the same, he was a natural said Patricia Arquette, who also talked him through some tips on undressing. 'He was amazing, but very strict who he undressed in front of. I think he energised everyone on set. In fact, he was as much a guiding force on the movie as Tim was. We had these very intimate scenes together, and he would get right into the part and stay there for hours. I'm not that disciplined. I still have fits of laughter during a scene, but Johnny could do it straight.'

The attention to detail was just as essential a part of the filming itself. Under the watchful eye of designer Tom Duffield, building identical sets for Wood's ultra low-budget movies was the most challenging. Each one, he remembers, far exceeded the cost that Wood probably spent on all his movies put together. 'The hardest thing was to not make anything look nice. Items we couldn't find we had to build. Ed's sets were made from inexpensive things he threw together, but our sets were hand-crafted, tailor-made, and far from cheap.'

Burton also took pains to highlight the film's autobiographical nature, pulling in elements of 68 different locations, many of which were, in fact, Wood's own past stomping grounds. 'It was a vibrant shoot,' recalls Johnny. 'I mean, it was really tough because we were filming in some of the most claustrophobic, badly ventilated, most uncomfortable locations in Hollywood. My adrenalin was pumping all the way, but everyone from the ground up was giving the movie 200 per cent.' That is why, he explained, it was the most ensemble picture he had yet made. 'I don't think I've worked on anything where everyone was so close knit.'

Wood's second wife Kathy, too, was equally effusive in her praise of the film and, in particular, of Johnny's performance. They didn't meet until Kathy decided to visit the location filming. Johnny remembers how nervous he was as she watched him playing her husband. 'It was a real eye-opener for the part. She gave me Edward's wallet and his phone book. I was initially a little fazed by it because I really didn't know how to take it. But it really took the sting out of meeting someone who really knew the person you are playing on film. The wallet and the phone book became real important to the way that I finally fleshed out the part.'

With such high praise, it should be no surprise that Johnny was looking forward to watching the finished film. In fact, it was the first time he'd felt comfortable about seeing something he was in. 'I'm really excited as it was such a great experience. The whole time we were doing it, it felt like a really good departure from any of the other shit that I've done.'

More importantly, Johnny admitted later, 'Ed was someone who was not afraid to take chances and did exactly what he wanted to do. He did the best he could do with what was available to him and he was able to put together images that were surreal, with moments of genius, I think. His movies were all his and they were genuine. I hope Ed is remembered as an artist.' Not only that, continued Johnny, 'but I thought it would be nice to make a film that was a real love letter to him, and to try to clean up what filth had been thrown on his name.' That is certainly how he played the part.

In fact, it was strangely ironic that only a few months after the film was released, Johnny joined Disney and the other principals from the movie in a campaign to have a star placed on Hollywood Boulevard. He was 'trying to get Eddie a star on the Walk of Fame, because it's important. Someone said there's a star next to Bela Lugosi that's available.' That, said Johnny, 'would just be perfect',

Ed Wood opened in America in October 1994 to excellent reviews despite its less-than-mediocre box office. Writing in *Entertainment Weekly*, Richard Corliss called Johnny 'an exemplary actor who can't do much more than smile heroically in the face of every humiliation.' *Première* magazine shared those sentiments: 'Depp plays Wood as a wide innocent caught up in the illusions of cinema. He's another *Edward Scissorhands*. He looks petrified with glee throughout the film,' and the *Village Voice* said much the same by adding that the film was 'flawlessly crafted — as fastidious as any previous Burton production.'

In Britain, where the movie was released in the following May, the reception was much the same. *Empire* magazine had no doubts whatsoever about Johnny's portrayal. 'Depp gives a truly mesmerising performance, both in and out of drag, notching up another distinctly oddball role that again reveals the measure of the young actor's talents. A sublime treat.'

Indeed, *Ed Wood* was Johnny's third movie to earn him a Golden Globe nomination, again for Best Comedic Actor. More importantly, for the film itself, it walked away with two Oscars at the 1995 Academy Awards ceremony. One for Best Make-Up and one for Martin Landau, for Best Actor, for his portrayal of Bela Lugosi.

Interestingly enough, seven months later, Johnny would purchase Lugosi's old home, or The Castle as it is still known, for a reputed $2.3 million. It was situated on a 2.5-acre plot of land near Hollywood's Sunset Strip with walls and gates surrounding its 9,000 sq ft estate. It had been owned since 1980 by celebrated Hollywood divorce lawyer Marvin Mitchelson, who had been forced to sell it following his conviction for tax fraud 13 years later.

'It's great,' Johnny still raves to this day. 'Lugosi lived in it in the Forties; they shot part of the *Wizard of Oz* there, and those things are very interesting titbits, nice to know. But I just love the house, it's such a strange design, very unusual architecture. It's like a weird little castle in the middle of Hollywood, but I'm hardly ever there.' But Mr Pink, as Johnny calls him, is always on hand.

'He's a friend of mine who lives in the house and takes care of the property. I don't know why he's called that. For 25 years he has been Mr Pink. He used to work with Pink Floyd and it would make sense if it was because of that. He's a good guy. If I lived there alone, the place would be a wreck. They'd call in the health department. There's no way I could take care of all that stuff myself. Mr Pink is great, sort of a good friend who just takes care of everything.'

But he wasn't the only resident. Years later, Johnny turned his mind towards bizarre garden furniture again. He began looking for something unusual to place in his front yard. By 1997, he came across the ideal piece — an 8ft yellow gorilla. 'He comes from *Fear and Loathing*,' laughed Johnny. 'He's got the words "You Can Run But You Cannot Hide" emblazoned on his stomach. I saw him and fell in love with him, as one does with an 8ft gorilla, and I thought,

"Aah, I've got a good idea. I'll rig him up for those bastard neighbours who've been complaining about the construction and fucking leaves in their garden." That was horrible shit.'

As Johnny himself would point out, 'they're real trainspotters, real nit-pickers. I had the construction crew on the film build his hand so he was flicking the bird (giving the finger). He also has a giant erection; we built a pump into him so he's constantly peeing into a bucket. The neighbours haven't commented yet, but they must know he was put there for them. I've had him moved now, but he used to stand facing their little veranda where they sit and have coffee every morning. Now he's right at the end of my driveway, so just as you park your car there's this enormous gorilla with a giant hard-on — welcome to Johnny's.'

Aside from Mr Pink, there was also Moo, Johnny's pitbull terrier, a present from Kate. 'He doesn't bite. That's just the propaganda against pitbulls. It depends what the owner's like. I don't bite too hard either. I miss him when I'm away. I also have two Rottweilers, called Red and Black. So it's Moo, Pink, Red, Black and me. I don't have a colourful name yet. I'm looking forward to one, though.'

From *Ed Wood*, Johnny moved on to shooting *Don Juan DeMarco*, a movie that advance reports insisted would prove as uproarious as its predecessor was outrageous. The idea was the brainchild of Jeremy Levin whose 1990's screenplay was loosely based on Lord Byron's mythical character of the same name. 'I always wanted to do a movie about women, love, romance and sex,' explained Levin. 'And I always wondered whether anyone had done a movie about Don Juan.' They hadn't.

Not only that, continues Levin, but 'Byron's piece is a

very long tome that has a tremendous amount of politics, but some absolutely wonderful scenes. I freely appropriated some of these scenes, and then worked them into a screenplay about another issue.' That other issue was his own personal experiences as a psychotherapist and his fascination with Don Juan.

Born and raised in Woodbridge, Connecticut, Levin's career had been pre-ordained since his primary school days; even then, he was dedicated to writing in one form or another. Pursuing his interest, he published two novels: *Creator* and *Satan: His Psychotherapy and Cure, By The Unfortunate Dr Kassler, JSPS*. Later, he founded and directed *The Proposition*, a satirical theatre group which he ran in Cambridge, Massachusetts for ten years and off-Broadway for a further four. Over the following years, he worked as a television director, school teacher, state hospital psychologist, Harvard University faculty member, and a clinical physiologist before moving into writing and directing films in 1980 with the screen adaptation of his own novel, *Creator*, and another, *Playing For Keeps.*

For his *Don Juan DeMarco* screenplay he introduced psychiatrist Jack Mickler (Marlon Brando) as the catalyst for his exploration of the grey area between fantasy and reality. After nearly 30 years of listening, encouraging and unravelling other people's miseries, he is all but burnt out. He has little left for either his colleagues or his long-suffering wife, played by Faye Dunaway. He is simply living out the emotions of someone awaiting imminent retirement.

That is until Don Juan DeMarco provides him with the most intriguing and fascinating case of his career.

Indeed, DeMarco's tales of love and passion are exactly what Mickler needs to restore his professional etiquette and flagging marriage.

The opening sequence wastes no time introducing the main character, a young man perched precariously on the narrow catwalk at the top of an advertising billboard 40 feet above street level. With his face hidden by a mask, cloaked in flowing cape, and wielding a raised sabre, the figure claims to be Don Juan (Johnny), the world's greatest lover, and the seducer of at least 1,500 women, but he is distraught. And he has every reason to be.

Although he has loved an almost countless number of women, the one woman he actually does love has rejected him. Convincing himself there is nothing, or no one left to love, suicide seems to be the most promising option. Promising that is until Dr Mickler bursts into his enclosed world of angst-ridden self-pity and succeeds where police officers have failed in talking the cloaked madman down from his suicidal perch.

Even on the fringe of professional retreat, Mickler swiftly decides he has nothing to lose by evaluating his now seemingly disillusioned patient with a ten-day course of diagnosis and treatment. Mickler is as delusive as his patient is distraught, and Don Juan takes his new mentor through a series of stories that are at best nothing more than wild erotic adventures. Everything from a childhood in a small Mexican town, a journey to Arabia where he is secretly pressed into service in a harem and an eventual shipwreck which washes him up on to a desert island to encounter his one true love, only to be rejected for openly admitting his past promiscuities.

Needless to say, Mickler, drawn into DeMarco's sagas of love, passion, and romance — strikingly photographed in gorgeous, colourful flashback sequences — finds himself restoring his already flagging marriage as a result of his patient's revelations.

Indeed, confirmed Levin, *Don Juan DeMarco* is a light, fantasy confection of a movie. And who better for the title role than Johnny? Although at the time of finishing his screenplay, the director had no preconceived ideas about an actor to play the part. 'I was told Johnny wanted to do it, and Don Juan as Johnny plays him is someone who's just unmitigatedly in love with love. Whether or not he's the real thing is inconsequential. He causes a tremendous transformation in Mickler.'

On a practical level, of course, many considered Johnny's haunting good looks suitably Latin for Don Juan. Mark Salisbury writing in *Empire* magazine couldn't agree more. 'It's a role Depp was born to play; his beauteous looks and doe-eyes are the perfect accompaniments to a lifetime of seduction and loving.'

Although Johnny was now firmly committed to the idea of filming *Don Juan DeMarco*, there was still one more bridge to cross. He would only appear in the film if Marlon Brando agreed to play the psychiatrist. At that point, Levin was worried. 'I thought the project was dead in the water, only to receive a second shock, hearing that Marlon was, in fact, interested.'

But then again, he knew Johnny loved the script. 'It's incredible writing,' Johnny still proclaims. 'My character's dialogue is so poetic and beautiful. The challenge for me was creating a character who was slightly cocky and noble, but likeable. I needed to create someone who has a strong sense of himself, but is still lost.'

The other thing, of course, was the fact that if Johnny was to have a hero or personal god it would be Brando. More importantly, the now ageing star was also Johnny's favourite actor, and to have the opportunity to work alongside him was like a dream come true. That's not to say Johnny's name alone wasn't enough to green-light the movie. Far from it. What was uncertain, however, was whether he had the clout to attract an actor of Brando's reputation to what could be considered a typically stereotyped, Johnny Depp oddball movie. Apparently, he did.

Brando himself, of course, more controversial than not during his 40-year career, had made 35 films, and could be said to have influenced much of the screen charisma Johnny now exuded, in much the same way as James Dean and Elvis Presley. Nominated seven times for Academy Awards as Best Actor, Brando had won twice, once in 1954 for *On the Waterfront*, and again in 1972 for his remarkable performance as Vito Corleone in Francis Ford Coppola's *The Godfather*. In doing so, he created a body of work that stands proud in its integrity, everything from *A Streetcar Named Desire*, *Viva Zapata!* and *Julius Caesar* to *The Wild One*, *Mutiny on the Bounty*, the controversial *Last Tango in Paris*, and, of course, his 15-minute cameo appearance in Christopher Reeves' *Superman: The Movie*.

Equally inspirational was the casting of Faye Dunaway in the pivotal role of Brando's wife. She, too, was thoroughly enamoured with Brando. 'He's an idol, a dream. He's a myth to every working actor in the world. And Johnny's a close second.'

'It was tremendously exciting working with Marlon and Faye,' Johnny recalls. 'They are actors with incredible careers. I was privileged to work alongside them and learn.' If he was assailed by self-doubt for any reason, within hours the tension, the nervousness, and perhaps the feeling of a star-struck boy from Kentucky soon fell away. 'You just jump in,' he adds, 'I was real nervous on my way over to his house. Then, as soon as I saw him, he just instantly, magically, put me at ease within seconds of saying "Hello". He became this great wonderful guy I was working with. He was a big, big factor in me doing the film.'

It was something producer Patrick Palmer noticed as well. 'Let's face it, we've got the most talented actor over the age of 60, the most talented actor under the age of 30, and one of the most acclaimed actresses in Hollywood.'

And he was right. In fact, the reviews for the film couldn't have been better if Levin had written them himself. 'I wanted *Don Juan* to be about so many things — about what's important in life, and the connection between people. It's a story about life beginning again, about humanity and the way we're all living. Most importantly, it's about staying alive in life.'

The critics agreed. The movie was utterly delightful, the general consensus ran — 'Johnny Depp stands up to Brando as the best young actor in Hollywood. The part seems made for him, and he plays it without narcissism or camp,' wrote Derek Malcolm in *The Guardian*.

Another raved, 'Depp seems permanently drawn to characters on the fringe of society and is perfectly cast as a man who takes boyish delight in the opportunities that life possesses.'

Again it was high praise for another of Johnny's oddball outsider roles, but maybe Johnny was rapidly tiring of playing the oddball outsider. Maybe, too, it was time for that blockbuster action movie that he had so proudly avoided through his previous work. Certainly there were those critics who wanted to make him painfully aware of that. Johnny, however, remained adamant. 'I'm not blockbuster boy. I never wanted to be.'

Besides, he continues, 'you can never predict what's going to be commercial but I have to feel stimulated by the material in order to turn in a good performance. I'm not going to take the dull character for the sake of a big pay cheque. It's very easy to take that road, but there's just ... nothing there, you know. Everything has been done ten zillion times and if you can, at least, try for something a little different, then why not? I just want to do the things I want to do.'

CHAPTER 10

'I've never liked being in the public eye.
It makes me feel very uncomfortable.
That's why I love spending time in Paris
so much. I can do what I want without being
scrutinised, judged or stalked. I'm not really
interested in glitz. I prefer to live a life filled
as much as possible with unusual experiences.'

The Nick Of Time

Johnny and Kate left for the Cannes Film Festival shortly before *Ed Wood* and *Don Juan DeMarco* were released in America in May 1995 to attend the première of his next movie, Jim Jarmusch's *Dead Man*.

Jarmusch, of course, like Tim Burton, could be described as one of the few visionary directors to have established himself in the upper echelons of Hollywood. A former film student, he first came to the public's attention in 1984 with his low-budget black-and-white piece, *Stranger than Paradise*, and then two years later with *Down by Law*. But he is probably best known, however, for his obliquely observed study of foreign tourists adrift after hours in Elvis-haunted Memphis in 1989's *Mystery Train*, and for his stunningly visualised *Night on Earth* three years later. The latter takes his audience on five cab rides in five cities over the course of a single night, linked by the interaction of passengers and drivers, one played by Winona Ryder. Interestingly enough, though, it is perhaps one of his least-seen movies. It certainly was from Winona's point of view.

So with that pedigree, it should be no surprise that Johnny wanted to link up with the acclaimed cult director even though the film opened to generally bemused critical reaction. It was, noted some, a hypnotic, slow moving, sometimes astonishing western, that seemed to have much more in common with Ingmar Bergman's *The Seventh Seal* and Sam Shephard's mystical western *Silent Tongue* from 1993 — River Phoenix's last film — than it had with any characteristic Hollywood outing. Maybe that was *Dead Man*'s greatest downfall, in critical terms at least. Derek Malcom thought so when he wrote his review for *The Guardian*; 'What looks like an intriguing short story is stretched by Jarmusch into over two hours of slow burning and effortful watching, with its humour existing side by side with a kind of portentous visual philosophising.'

All the same, its glorious black-and-white photography — stunningly shot by Robert Muller — made the film an intriguing and nicely paced contemporary western epic with a dash of classic *film noir* thrown in for good measure.

For Jarmusch as well as Johnny, it was, according to the press release, the story of a young man's journey, both physically and spiritually, into very familiar territory. William Blake (Johnny) travels to the extreme western frontiers of America some time in the second half of the nineteenth century. Lost and badly wounded, he encounters a very odd, outcast Native American named Nobody (Gary Farmer), who believes Blake is actually the dead English poet of the same name.

The story, with Nobody's help, leads Blake through situations that are in turn comical and violent. Contrary to his nature, circumstances transform Blake into a hunted outlaw, a killer, and a man whose physical existence is slowly slipping away. Thrown into a world that is cruel and chaotic, his eyes are opened to the fragility that defines the realm of the living. It is as though he passes through the surface of a mirror, and emerges into a previously unknown world that exists on the other side.

Johnny adored the movie, and the character he was playing even more so. At the same time, though, he hoped it was 'the last of these innocents I play. It's a character that is, again, like a naïve young guy who's trying to get his life together. He's trying really hard to make his life work and he ends up slowly dying. And he knows he's dying. It's a beautiful story, though.'

In fact, Jarmusch wrote the part of William Blake with Johnny in mind. Not surprising, really, since he was a friend, and by the time filming got under way, he had been for five years. 'He really is one of the most precise and focused people I've ever worked with,' enthused the director of his star. 'The whole crew was kind of amazed by that. It's a side of him that I'm not really familiar with. I'm more familiar with seeing him fall asleep on the couch with the TV on all night. But it somehow fits; he's full of paradoxes.

'What I love about him as an actor is his subtlety and very interesting physicality, which is underplayed; he has amazing eyes, which he uses to great effect. I didn't appreciate his precision until I worked with him; he doesn't make false moves or overdo it.'

Much the same as Robert Mitchum, one of America's most accomplished actors of the western genre, who had four years earlier returned to the screen for a cameo role in Martin Scorsese's *Cape Fear* — the director's gripping remake of Mitchum's 1962 original.

Johnny was also thoroughly enamoured to be working with him, particularly when he would recall Mitchum's 'Love' and 'Hate' tattooed fingers from Charles Laughton's *The Night of the Hunter*, the same one to which Winona had introduced him, long before it was restored by the British Film Institute in 1999. Today, Johnny still values the experience. 'He was about 7ft tall and in great shape. He's a tough guy.'

That was something Johnny could comprehend, in retrospect at least. Painfully aware of his public profile, he believed that to many people he was a celebrity first and an actor a poor second, and that his career, his work and even his personality were being judged accordingly.

Public perception of Johnny was influenced by such apparently inconsequential remarks as his curiosity with the afterlife. Nowhere was that better expressed than when staying at the Mackay Mansion in Nevada during filming. It was a three-storey Victorian house reputedly haunted by a little girl wearing a silk party dress with a blue sash. 'I want to run into some spirits here,' he told *Première* magazine.

'When I was a kid, I used to have these dreams. But they weren't dreams. I was awake, but I couldn't move. I couldn't speak. And a face would come to me. Someone told me it was the spirit of someone who died that was very close and never got to say something that they wanted to say. And I believe it.' And that wouldn't be the only occasion he would openly admit to such experiences.

'I was staying at this hotel in London that used to be a hospital. This face, like an evil surgeon's face, suddenly came right at me. I was just lying in bed, and I was asleep and wasn't on any sort of drugs. It really scared me, which was cool.'

Not so cool was the time he stayed in Paris, in the room where Oscar Wilde died. 'I didn't see him. It was definitely the bed he died in. I'm not sure if it was the room, but there was all his furniture. I was a little paranoid that I might be buggered by his ghost at 4.00am.'

One of the biggest thrills for Johnny, however, was the time he visited the home of escapologist Harry Houdini, situated above Laurel Canyon. Although now a collection of ruins, 'Canyon residents tell of strange happenings on the hilltop site. There's no house. I bet this was a really romantic place at night. I often think I might have been Houdini myself at one time.' And it's no coincidence that Winona Ryder used to buy him antique locks for what he called his 'Houdini' hobby.

He also thought it was time to extend his range of movie roles. It was a realisation that surfaced towards the end of *Don Juan DeMarco* and now he wanted to make it happen.

John Badham's latest project seemed ideal, and Johnny was hooked when he heard what the director was filming. All the same, it seemed strange that Badham should take on a third remake of Alfred Hitchcock's **1934** *The Man*

Who Knew Too Much. Strange, that is, when you consider it was one of Hitchcock's best-loved thrillers, and even spawned another version, updated and colour-enhanced by the director himself 22 years later.

For the Hitchcock audience, the story centred on a young girl kidnapped to prevent her parents from revealing their knowledge of a political assassination plot. But in attempting to find a new angle for Badham's 1995 version, *Nick of Time*, the plot was twisted slightly by turning the central role into a young professional who is forced to carry out the political assassination himself to save his young daughter's life. Even in pre-production, the forthcoming *Nick of Time* promised to be a tantalising remake of the Hitchcock original.

It all starts on a normal afternoon for accountant Gene Watson (Johnny) as time ticks by without incident. But not for long. He is about to become entangled in one of those high-octane dramas that holds the general population gripped when played out on the news. Fate has just dealt him a terrifying hand.

Arriving at Union Station in downtown Los Angeles for an appointment, Gene and his six-year-old daughter Lynn, played by Courtney Chase, are suddenly taken hostage by police impostors Christopher Walken and Roma Maffia (aka Mr Smith and Mr Jones). Gene is told he must commit a murder within the next 90 minutes or his daughter will die. Any effort Watson makes to go to the authorities is stymied by the sure knowledge that the kidnappers will retaliate by carrying out their threat. In his frantic race against the clock, each moment has immediate and deadly consequences.

The fact of being at the wrong place at the wrong time lies at the heart of the movie. Certainly that is true for Johnny's character Gene Watson. He is confronted with the most profound and frightening situation imaginable. An 'ordinary' accountant and devoted father whose courage and wits are tested in a unique, harrowing ordeal. It appears that the kidnappers' insane and compelling plan will implicate Watson through a home video in which he will appear to be an unhinged loner hell-bent on exacting a terrible revenge.

As John Badham, best known for *Saturday Night Fever* and *Blue Thunder* explains, 'Nearly every day the newspaper reports incredible but true incidents that are as unfathomable as they are tragic. Such stories repeatedly demonstrate that truth is much stranger than fiction. Most people expect each day of the week to unfold much like the one before. Yet every single day there are those who will experience something so unexpected or shocking that they can't even accept the fact that it is happening, and it's happening to them.'

That, he continues, 'is the situation faced by Johnny's character — an ordinary man who gets caught up in extraordinary circumstances that are horrible and beyond his control. This situation could happen to any of us. *Nick of Time* puts before the filmgoer the terrifying question, "What would *you* do if this happened to you?"'

From that point of view, it was easy to understand Johnny's attraction to the role. It not only offered him the opportunity to distance himself from the kind of roles he had played for the last five years — the oddball or kooky — but it could also be seen as a calculated attempt to shake off any last vestiges of what his critics called his 'quirky' typecasting.

Executive producer DJ Caruso agreed. 'His role is very different from what we've seen Johnny do in the past, and the audience will be rooting for him even as they wonder whether he can be the hero.'

That is certainly how Johnny played the part. Even the stunts were 90 per cent his own, everything from the elaborate fight sequences to the daring 90ft cable fall. 'Action actor' was how stunt co-ordinator Shane Dixon acknowledged Johnny's resilience in his determination to succeed — and he did that as well.

There was, however, another factor in Johnny's relish of the role. It tapped perfectly into his intense desire for a family of his own. It was an area of his private life which apparently caused difficulties in his relationship with Kate Moss as much as it had with Winona Ryder.

'To play the role, I drew on what was accessible,' Johnny confirmed. 'Family is very important to me. I have nieces and nephews whom I absolutely worship. If anything happened to them, I would go crazy and do anything to save them.'

Equally intriguing was the idea of teaming Johnny up with Christopher Walken. It was a stroke of genius on Badham's part, and another of Johnny's reasons for accepting the role. It would also help him to overcome any concerns he had for playing an action hero. Up until then, he thought he would 'look goofy as an action man unless I could wear a shirt that had "Action Man" printed on it, then I would do it'.

Shooting commenced on 2 April 1995 at the Westin

Bonaventure Hotel in the heart of downtown Los Angeles, just a few blocks away from Union Street. It was commandeered for several scenes, while a hotel shoe-shine stand and near-by plant shop were constructed with transparent glass and clocks were strategically placed to offer stark reminders that time for Johnny's character was running out.

Johnny would, according to Badham, arrive on set at 7.00am, sometimes not looking his best. 'We would start to stage a scene, and I would think he was only propped up by a stage brace. He would stand there looking quite shaken, but totally focused.' The director didn't even ask what Johnny may have been up to the night before. 'Why ask the obvious? What I learned right away was, it didn't matter if he never went to bed the night before, because he was right on top of it.' Evidence enough that this extraordinary young actor was also remarkably instinctive.

Johnny's co-star Gloria Reuben agreed, albeit for different reasons. 'He's a Gemini. Very sensitive, a little shy and very funny. If he wanted to trash a hotel room with me in it, that would be just fine.'

At the same time, Johnny also faced the challenge of filming the story in chronological order, as opposed to the more usual movie technique of shooting out of sequence, and then cutting it together at a later stage. The film, Badham explained, 'was shot as if we just happened upon these people and their circumstances. The actors were filmed without make-up using hand-held cameras to achieve a raw, realistic feeling.'

He elaborates. 'A documentary is shot with the knowledge that you have one shot to get it right, so you can't always put the camera exactly where you would like. You can't always be in focus. Sometimes you're too far or too close to the action. The lighting isn't always perfect or flattering to your subject. That is the illusion we tried to create.'

For Johnny, it was an inspiring and instructive process. 'We did a lot of scenes that involved two or three cameras, which reduced the number of takes and kept a freshness and spontaneity to the acting. You're not bound within frame lines and feel like you can go anywhere and do anything.'

All the same, continued Badham, 'You can't skip or take short cuts through transmissions and mundane aspects of a story, such as when a guy is seen leaving his office in one scene, and then walking through his front door in the next. In this situation, we have to stay with Johnny's character wherever he goes and at the same time, keep the pace moving.'

His enthusiasm for his performance, and his acceptance of the challenges he endured while filming *Nick of Time*, proved that Johnny could hold his own in any company and in any movie. It seemed only natural that having once played in the big action leagues, he would only continue there.

But there were some people, however, who were surprised, even shocked, at the news of his next film project.

Enjoying the freedom of being between movies, Johnny turned his attention to an aspect of his career that he had not yet pursued at any great length — directing his own feature. It was something he had long wanted to do. And nowhere is that desire better expressed than in the clutch of music videos he had directed for and with his own circle of friends and colleagues.

He shared the directing honours, for instance, for Red Hot Chilli Pepper John Frusciante's first album with Gibby Haynes; he directed another for Shane MacGowan and the Pogues; he appeared alongside them on *Top of the Pops*; and he even found time to direct a couple of film shorts, one a 12-minute journey through a house filled with junk backed by a rock 'n' roll soundtrack, and the other, an eight-minute anti-drug documentary. All of these could be seen as Johnny's yearning for his next project as director, star and writer of *The Brave*.

Well, not exactly *the* writer. Johnny had written the screenplay with his brother Dan, when the two adapted Gregory MacDonald's novel of the same name. 'It's about a man making a sacrifice for his family,' explained Johnny. 'And I play that man, and since I've sponged off and stolen as much as I can from the film-makers I've been fortunate enough to work with — Tim Burton, John Waters, Emir Kusturica, Lasse Hallstrom, Jim Jarmusch — I thought I'd try directing one myself. But I have absolutely no idea why. I felt somehow driven to it.'

Unfortunately, a lot of people disagreed with him intensely. Although Johnny was, by this time, an actor with a well-respected pedigree, this was his first major directorial project, and although it turned out to be a unique look at the sorry state of contemporary American Indian culture, Johnny certainly had his fair share of critics.

His idea, as one of those critics put it, 'was to pose a problem and he does this without once pausing to inject his work with feel-good amphetamines. If anything, *The*

Brave is designed to make the viewer feel as though he's sitting on a mat of needles — however much we squirm and shift, we just can't get away from those little points of pain.'

It was the classic, but also timeless, tale of redemption, about how an American Indian man, Raphael, played by Johnny, out of work and desperate for cash, decides to sell his life to a producer of 'snuff' films, played by Marlon Brando, whose work involves the filming of genuine and horrendously brutal murder scenes, for which he pays huge sums of money. Raphael accepts a 'role', so that his wife (Elpidia Carillo) and his children can have a more comfortable future. He has one week to report back to the set where the movie-makers will torture and kill him. The movie then centres on the seven days Raphael spends with his family, the first and last good days they will ever have together.

With only a few dollars in his pocket and even fewer days to live Raphael springs a number of surprises on his family. Probably the most successful is the scene when he builds a vast fun fair in the middle of the night that is almost unapologetically lifted from Johnny's own *Arizona Dream* movie. The only difference is that this time the construction is not a flying machine.

In another scene, Raphael is confronted by the producer's vile assistant, memorably played by Marshall Bell, who promptly plunges a pick-axe into his hand. Equally daunting is the opening sequence, when Raphael arrives at a deserted warehouse, is interviewed by the same unpleasant character, and is finally ushered to a subterranean chamber where an electric chair, and Brando in a wheelchair puffing on a mouth organ, await him.

Johnny's vision was certainly haunting, with the

viewer's discomfort multiplying as the story unfolds. There is, for instance, the inevitable brutality of Raphael's final 'starring' role. It appears that for a down-and-out American Indian, selling his body to die in a snuff movie is the only route available to secure a better way of life for his family. That theme lies at the heart of the movie. Raphael drinks, moves in and out of prison, and can't afford a car. His own family exist in a dilapidated village next to a waste dump in the middle of a deserted nowhere. There, like other similarly deprived sectors of society, they build their homes from pieces of scrap material and rummage through mounds of rubbish each day barely managing to get by.

Once again, Johnny was totally delighted to be working with Marlon Brando, even if he was only playing a cameo role. Far more important, Johnny concedes it was an act of friendship that left him completely floored. 'Marlon coming and doing this film for me was an incredible blessing. It was beyond a dream. I was very fortunate to have worked with him, and maintained a friendship, a relationship with him, so when we went to work together, the process was very enjoyable. We were cackling and laughing together.'

But as far as directing Brando went, Johnny wasn't remotely worried. 'I don't think anyone needs to direct him. You just turn the camera on and capture him, and take what you can take. What he came in and did for me was above and beyond anything I ever expected. He really dug inside.'

Even with Brando, the film seemingly did nothing more than gather dust on a distributor's shelf. But two years later, in May 1997, it was scheduled for its international début at Cannes. With so much conspiring against the film, the first reviews following its première came as a major shock. Many were disappointing. 'Every morbid, sensitive high school kid's dream movie,' wrote one US critic.

Another called it 'oddly haunting' for its eccentricity. 'There's a lot wrong with *The Brave*, with a pace that may be intended to evoke desert languor, but is often plain leaden. It wasn't the most narcisstic film a director has ever made starring himself.'

Some, however, were much kinder. Johnny Depp, wrote *The Guardian* critic Jonathan Romney, 'comes across as wanting to create his own cinematic style. Cannes catcalls not withstanding, he should be encouraged to give directing another go.'

Indeed, as Johnny himself explains, 'I was very naïve. I thought directing would be easy to do, but it's insane. Completely insane. You don't sleep when you're supposed to sleep, and when you're working, you're desperate to sleep. People ask you questions like "What colour would you like the red shoes to be?" when "red" would suffice. It's the most insane thing I've ever done.'

There was, of course, a temptation to draw comparisons with Kevin Costner's *Dances with Wolves*. Indeed, if Costner was praised for his use of ecological imagery, then Johnny had displayed a similar skill. American Indians, it seems, living on recycled material, taking public transportation, giving their children toys they made with their own hands, are an obvious tragedy, mainly because the American Indians 200 years ago were ecologists by choice and tradition. For the same people today, it's a condition enforced by poverty.

It was something Johnny's ex-fiancée Winona Ryder

understood as much as Johnny himself. She had, after all, been raised on a Californian commune with Northern California Indians as neighbours. It was, according to Winona, where the two cultures — emphasising community, simplicity and respect for the earth — were so similar that the lines between them often blurred.

'Native American culture is American culture,' Winona believes. 'And we can all learn from it. It's just so profoundly important to preserve all of our country's culture.' It is what led to her involvement with the American Indian College Fund to raise funds and maintain an interest in that same cultural heritage.

She even asked Johnny to show her the movie. According to the December 1997 French *Première* magazine, the last time they saw each other, Winona had been pleading with him. But it was impossible because the film was locked away in a safe.

But Winona also knew that the film had special meaning for Johnny. In a strange way, he was proud. 'I thought it sort of parallelled what happened to the American Indians 100 or more years ago.' Even more convincingly, elements of the movie echoed his own concern that he still considered America a gluttonous society that was all about winning and results, and again accused Andrew Jackson, the former President pictured on $20 bills, of being a genocidal murderer responsible for the death of millions of American Indians.

In fact, it was Johnny's appearance at Cannes that same year that publicly revealed something the Hollywood grapevine had been insisting for weeks — that he and Kate Moss had broken up. Within a month, Britain's *Sun* newspaper was reporting 'Supermodel Kate Moss has finally split from Hollywood hell-raiser Johnny Depp. The couple are going their separate ways after a stormy four-year relationship. A source said they planned to remain friends and Kate will go to Depp's film premières. Kate had once talked about marrying the *Edward Scissorhands* star. Earlier this year, Depp moved into Kate's New York flat. But instead of cementing the relationship, the couple found they got on each other's nerves.'

The *New York Post* said much the same. 'Things were already rocky for the couple back in May at the Cannes Film Festival. They rented separate villas. Kate shared one with her pals from Oasis. And they never visited each other's pad. Friends say Kate wants to keep the relationship alive, but Johnny won't change to suit her. When Depp was in town recently, the pair didn't even see each other once.' Johnny's spokeswoman, at the time, however, wasn't so sure. 'To our knowledge, the break-up is untrue.'

True or not, it didn't stop *People* magazine subsequently suggesting that 'According to friends, Moss wants to continue to date Depp occasionally, but Depp isn't into open relationships.' And in *New York* magazine, 'Kate has told friends that she called it quits with the hot-tempered heart-throb last week because they were having too many fights. They've had small separations before but this was a major break-up. '

Far more dubious was *Star* magazine's revelations by Janet Charlton that Winona Ryder had been calling Johnny because she still cared for him. Winona remained unperturbed by speculation, and the suggestion seemed preposterous.

Another report in the *New York Post*, however, was quick to notice that Kate did not remain alone for long. 'Moss has taken up with 32-year-old Tarka Cordell. Sources say that, for the past year, Cordell has stayed at Moss' apartment in New York whenever he's in town ... "To my knowledge, they've been friends for a while," says Paul Rowland, owner of Moss' agency, "but I don't think there's any romance involved."'

But Johnny was in no hurry to let anyone else into his life. Although Jennifer Love Hewitt of television's *Party of Five* would admit to having a crush on him, it was never suggested that they were a couple. Not even when he turned up on the set of her television series. That was more to do with a fan letter she had sent him years earlier.

'It was one of those days when I was dressed in sweats and wasn't wearing any make-up. I looked hideous. I was in my trailer when all of a sudden I hear the wardrobe girl yell "Johnny Depp is standing right outside." I just couldn't meet him looking so awful. So I ran out of the trailer, screaming at the top of my lungs until he left. I was totally humiliated.'

As for Kate, Johnny concedes, 'We would still be together today if I hadn't behaved like such an idiot. She was the best thing that ever happened to me, but I blew it because I was too moody and too miserable to be around. I hated myself and she couldn't take it any more. I don't blame her one bit. I would give anything to have Kate in my life again. I was sick to my stomach. I think anyone who has ever broken up with a girl he loves understands that. You're lying in bed, staring at your TV, smoking your fifth pack of cigarettes and wondering how you managed to make such a mess of a good thing.

'I still feel that way about Kate. She knows how I feel about her. But we also probably know there's no going back. If I could have taken things more easily and not got so depressed about my work and other garbage, we could have been so happy. I don't know, maybe I just couldn't deal with the fact that things were so good between us and had to act like an idiot and push her away.'

No sooner was his work on *The Brave* complete than Johnny was starting work on yet another movie. Joining Marlon Brando once again, Debra Winger, and *Dead Man* ally John Hurt, he headed out to County Cork, off the Irish coast, to film *Divine Rapture*, Thom Eberhardt's dark satire about religious miracles.

In fact, it was amusingly ironic that Johnny would be playing an investigative journalist looking into an assortment of miracles that Brando's character, the local priest, is apparently involved in. Winger was given the substantial role of a fisherman's wife who dies but is later brought back to life, and Hurt was cast as the local doctor.

Life on the set, however, was not without its dramas. It was barely the eighth week of location filming when the production first hit trouble, from the Irish Catholic Church of all places. Two of their churches, Eberhardt believed, had a sociological resonance essential to the movie's sense of realism. Unfortunately, the local clergy didn't see it that way. Nor did the Bishop of Clyne, who believed that churches were not film sets. As far as he was concerned, Ballycotton's Star of the Sea and Immaculate Conception churches could not be used. Not only that, but Brando's priest character was, in his opinion, an insult to Catholicism.

The locations, however, were not the only problems that Thom Eberhardt had to contend with as the *Divine Rapture* set hit even more trouble. 'I've been over here eight weeks already,' complained the director. 'Most of the time, the weather was glorious. Then as soon as we got under way the rain rolled in.'

Not that anyone could be blamed for thinking things weren't running smoothly. Quite the opposite, in fact. The villagers of Ballycotton welcomed the film crew enthusiastically. For them, the arrival of Hollywood film-makers could only mean one thing — dollars in their pockets. Even Marlon Brando's $4 million fee, they believed, would help the local economy. It did, for a time.

The actor began shopping for a place to stay. By the time production got under way in mid-July 1995, he had found one. A mansion in nearby Shanagarry for which the production would pay the owner $4,000 a week. 'I have never been so happy in my life.' Even when he stepped off the plane, 'I had this rush of emotion. I have never felt so at home in a place as I do here. I am seriously contemplating Irish citizenship.'

Although the shooting of the movie hit snag after snag, Johnny did, nonetheless, manage a couple of day's filming. Between takes, he was happy signing autographs, or at other times, he just sat in his room at the exclusive Ballymaloe House where he would be staying for the duration of the shoot. Although Kate was expected to join him, she didn't. In the end, his friend, and now *Batman* star, Val Kilmer flew out to join him.

Not that he would be staying long. Neither would Johnny for that matter. Three days later, and with only 20 minutes of shot footage, production on the movie was halted completely. The word around the set was that the less than moderate $16 million budget was washed up. Either that, or the film's financial backers Cinefin were deliberately pulling out of the project.

Although Brando had already been paid $1 million up front, Johnny and the rest of the cast and technical crew were less fortunate. Eberhardt was worried. 'Basically, what you have is a roomful of question marks and, upstairs, another roomful of producers where the problem now lies.'

For an entire week, work on *Divine Rapture* was suspended while those problems were thrashed out by the powers-that-be. Unfortunately, in the ensuing battle of wits, there was no winner. Production was officially halted. The cheques paid out the previous week were unlikely to be met and the seven years that Eberhardt had spent in development on the movie collapsed in just one weekend. A statement was issued.

'With deep regret, we have had to cease production of *Divine Rapture*. In spite of continuing assurance of financial backing, the funds have not been forthcoming. Along with cast and crew, we are shocked at the situation and deeply saddened by our inability to continue with this wonderful project. We wish to thank the people of Ballycotton who showed us so much support, and we will be doing everything we can to compensate them for their time and effort.'

But the cast and crew were not the only ones out of pocket. Fishermen, hoteliers and food suppliers all had outstanding bills that needed settlement. The Bay View Hotel, for instance, where much of the cast and crew stayed, was due payments for at least 20 rooms.

Even more damaging, long after the actors went home, was the aftermath of the film's failure. 'We hoped it would keep the hotels and guest houses full for years when the fame of the area spread throughout the world because of the film,' explained hotelier John O'Brien. Even Adrian Knowles, the owner of the Shanagarry mansion, was disappointed. Not only that, but he was another to suffer financially. 'I did receive a cheque that I understand will not be honoured, but I have been assured that I will be paid.'

It was a promise Brando himself made before his departure, long after Johnny had already given up hope on the production when it was first suspended. A weekend trip to France with Kate did not see him return.

'*Divine Rapture*,' Johnny laughs at the memory today. 'You want my experience of it? I had gotten a script from Marlon. He said, "Hey, come over and join me in Ireland. We'll do this thing. It'll be fun." I said, "Sure." I went over. We started shooting and were having a great time. Everything was real good. The next thing we knew, they were saying, "It's over." And that was it. It was like being in the middle of good sex, and then having the lights turned on and 15 people with machine-guns come in and say, "Stop or die." '

Meanwhile, Barry Navidi, one of the producers, predicted years of legal action between the producers and the financiers over the film's collapse. Far more important, he recalls, was the tragedy of it all. 'We have quite amazing rushes of the movie with incredible performances from the stars.' Mark Crowdy, one of the other producers, agreed with that summation.

After *Rapture*, Johnny's next role came knocking just as he was getting used to the freedom of being between movies. His agent thought it was perfect for him as she handed over the script of *Donnie Brasco*, Paul Attanasio's screenplay based on the book by Joseph D Pistone. Johnny quickly agreed.

CHAPTER 11

'Maybe one day I'll make a movie that really
blows people away. The sort of movie that I
can point to one night when I'm real old and
watching TV and say to my grandchildren:
"Hey, guys, Grandpop was pretty cool in this
film don,t you think?" Yeah — I'd like to be
able to say that about myself one day.'

In Love With Loathing

Five days into his stay with Hunter S Thompson, Johnny longs to sleep. Thompson, the self-styled King of Gonzo journalism and noted author of 1971's *Fear and Loathing In Las Vegas* is not a man noted for keeping regular hours. Like some kind of nocturnal vampire, he would live by night and then, finally, in the late afternoon, trail off to bed for a few hours before rising again. At that moment, Johnny would escape to the basement room, or 'the dungeon' as it's known, at Thompson's isolated Aspen retreat, still exhausted from Hunter's display of tireless excess, knowing that in a very short time the writer would be hammering on the door, yelling for him to get up.

After a couple of days, Johnny recalls, 'I began to

appreciate more and more that sleep was my friend. I was staying in the dungeon and it was the darkest room in the house. I'd go down there and lie on the bed, just rest up and read a book and smoke a cigarette. I really needed that time just to recharge before facing Hunter again.'

All the same, Johnny continues, 'He was incredibly generous to let me live in his basement. I spent the first week absorbing as much as I could by staying holed up with nothing but his books and my roll-ups for company. On the sixth day, I suddenly realised the room was packed with gunpowder kegs and I was smoking. I was lucky not to have blown the whole house up. Hunter just laughed when I told him.'

That was two years after the two men first met at the Woody Creek Tavern in Aspen, Colorado, Thompson's favourite drinking haunt. It was Johnny's, too. During his Christmas stay when taking a break from filming, he journeyed out to the ski resort with Kate, her mother and some others for a few days off. What he didn't expect was for Thompson to walk in, Johnny recalls, 'with a Taser gun in his left hand and a huge cattle prod in his right hand, swinging them around getting people out of his way.'

Neither did he expect him to take a seat at Johnny's table, to swap tales about their Kentucky roots; Johnny on Owensboro, Thompson on Louisville. He was even more surprised when he invited Johnny and his party back to his 'fortified compound' to carry on drinking. That compound, it turns out, had enough explosives, small fire-arms, canned food, bottled water and alcohol to survive even the aftermath of a nuclear war.

It was where Johnny's intense interest in the nickel-plated shotgun hanging on Thompson's wall turned to sheer delight. Surprisingly, Johnny recalls, 'He took it down and led me into the kitchen. He had a couple of big tanks of propane in there and handed me some nitro-glycerine capsules. We taped them to the side of the tank, took it out back, and I shot it. I've shot guns since I was eight years old, so I knew I could hit something.

'The target itself — a tube of nitro-glycerine — was pretty small, but the shotgun sprays, so I knew I'd hit something near. But I was kind of like, "I hope I don't miss." And bang! Boof! Bullseye! I got it first shot. There was this 75ft burst of fire, an enormous explosion. It was great fun. I was a little worried about shrapnel, but no one got caught, thank God. Mrs Moss was a little freaked out, but she did well. She hung in there, and when we left, she was kinda like, "Who is that man?"'

That man, it turned out, would be the basis for Johnny's next character on screen, or rather Thompson's alter-ego, Raoul Duke, in the movie version of *Fear and Loathing in Las Vegas*, the Thompson novel that was also Johnny's favourite book.

It was based on a journey that Thompson took with a friend, lawyer Oscar Zeta Acosta, to cover a road race, the Mint 400, for *Sports Illustrated*. 'My idea,' Thompson explained later, 'was to buy a fat notebook and record the whole thing as it happened, then send in the notebook for publication, without editing. But this is a hard thing to do and in the end I found myself imposing an essentially fictional framework on what began as a piece of straight/crazy journalism. As true "Gonzo" journalism, [a style of reporting based on William Faulkner's idea that the best fiction is far more true than any kind of other journalism] this doesn't work at all, and even if it did, I couldn't possibly admit it. Only a goddamned lunatic would write a thing like this and claim it was true.'

First published in *Rolling Stone* magazine under Raoul Duke's name, the magazine promptly gave the game away by revealing Thompson as the author. The initial piece, and the book that followed, was a landmark. A dark and idiosyncratic commentary on what Thompson called 'The Foul Year of Our Lord, 1971'.

By this time, of course, the Sixties had already ended. Nixon was in the White House, the war in Vietnam was still grinding on, the aftermath of the Beatles break-up was prolonged by one of the most disruptive earthquakes in the history of southern California, and it seemed the spirit of free thinking, free love and free drugs, once the buzzwords of a generation, were dead and buried.

Indeed, the Seventies had already begun to undo everything its predecessor had fought so hard for. The spirit of peace and love was pronounced dead at Altamont during a free Rolling Stones concert at a motor speedway arena just outside San Francisco, where a young black man was stabbed to death by Hell's Angels, stage centre, to the tune of 'Sympathy for the Devil', and captured in *Gimme Shelter*, a movie 'coming to a theatre near you' in 1971. The peace, love and innocence of Woodstock was history.

Dead, too, were Jimi Hendrix, Janis Joplin and Jim Morrison, three 27-year-old icons of rock 'n' roll, gone within the space of a year, all attributed to drug overdoses, and in a secret meeting with President Nixon, Elvis Presley offered his personal services as an undercover narcotics agent.

Good news for many was the death sentence for Charles Manson and three of his girl-gang members for the Tate–LaBianca murders, which had augured the apocalyptic end of flower power in 1969. Sixties' idealism had fast turned to cynicism, and the American dream was swiftly becoming the American nightmare.

Johnny agreed about the themes of Thompson's writing. 'What America was, what it might have been, what it's become now. Although the book is hysterically funny, it's written totally seriously; it's kind of melancholy. It's about the death of the American dream, the death of hope. At that time, Martin Luther King had been murdered, Robert and John F Kennedy had been murdered, there was a gangster in the White House. It was a really weird time. And it's only gotten weirder. I mean, we've recently been scrutinising the specifics of what the President has done with his penis.'

And he was right. Just as it must have seemed right that the only sane direction for Thompson to go was the one he took. Straight over the top and call it 'Gonzo'. That's certainly the route he took when he wrote *Fear and Loathing in Las Vegas* in 1971.

'That's when it all started,' recalls Thompson,'when I left Vegas for the first time, skipping the hotel bill, driving off in the red convertible all alone, drunk and crazy, back to LA. That's exactly what I felt. Fear and loathing.'

Although critically acclaimed for its literary success for nearly a quarter of a century, it had strangely remained untouched by Hollywood ever since. Strange, that is, when you consider the number of other great works that Hollywood has been involved with, but it could be that the money men considered Thompson's *Fear and Loathing* more difficult than most to bring to the screen. After all, just how do you translate page after page of drug-fuelled madness and paranoia, and bring it to life on celluloid? More important, of course, was finding the right film-maker to do it.

Almost 25 years later, British director Alex Cox, best known for *Repo Man* and *Sid and Nancy*, thought he had the answer. Armed with script and a respectable $5 million budget, he initially approached Johnny to ask him if he was interested in playing the part of Duke/Thompson. He was. Far more important for Johnny, of course, was the seal of approval from Thompson himself. He got that as well.

Cox also got Benicio Del Toro, best known for his role in *The Usual Suspects*, to play Thompson's road companion, Dr Gonzo. He then left for Aspen to meet with Thompson himself. That meeting, however, soon fell on stony ground. Thompson's idea of a fun-filled day that included placing a blow-up sex doll covered in film blood near the side of the road to mark the turning to his house didn't enthral Cox at all. Neither did the sausages Thompson cooked, or the ball game he wanted to watch on TV. 'Jesus Christ,' recalls the author. 'It was a classic example of how not to work, as a director, with writers. First he hated football, refused to watch it, and then I cooked really good sausages, which I prize, and he complained that he was vegetarian.'

Not long after, Cox surrendered his role as director over what the industry deemed as artistic differences of opinion, but another version credited Johnny with the coup. It wasn't until the arrival of Terry Gilliam taking over the director's seat that things improved.

From the outset, Gilliam seemed perfect. The choice

was understandable, too, for his career path endorsed his credibility. He had been an audacious interpreter of twentieth, and other, century manners, from *12 Monkeys* to *The Fisher King*, and from *The Adventures of Baron Munchausen* to *Brazil*, *The Time Bandits*, and the Monty Python trilogy.

More importantly, he had the ability to create the impossible on film with a vision that seemed to echo Tim Burton's same defiance of logic. On that point alone, it should be no surprise that Gilliam wanted to work with Johnny, and Johnny with Gilliam.

In fact, it turned out to be the prime reason the director accepted the project in the first place. 'I think Johnny is the best actor of his generation,' he confirmed. 'It was really a combination of the subject matter and Johnny that drove me to it. I don't think there's anything that Johnny can't do. He's very inventive, fast on his feet, funny and incredibly hard working.'

The feeling was apparently mutual. 'Terry came in, grabbed it, shook it around and did it right. He's one of the best directors I've ever worked with, one of the most inventive, pure, organic experiences that I've had. He'll give you a piece of direction, it sparks something in you, and boom, there's a huge explosion or flurry of creativity.'

Still, it was strange the way it came together, Gilliam continues. 'They were basically going to make a $5 million film with Alex Cox directing it. Then Johnny got involved and said, "This isn't enough money to make this film." So the budget crept up to $7 million.

'So they had a script, they had Johnny, and they had $7 million, but they didn't have a director, and so they came to me. I said, "OK. I'll come on. But we'll write a new script and I think you had better double the budget." I think we made it for about $18.5 million in the end.'

Johnny was thrilled. He had found a movie he was interested in, and a director he was interested in making it with. Now, he determined, he would observe Thompson at work and at play by spending three months with the writer at his Colorado home in Woody Creek. On one occasion, he even became 'Ray', his road manager and head of security for a book tour. Not so captivating, however, was arranging the bottle of Chivas and ice, which were required at every stop among other things. Afterwards, Johnny concedes, 'I wouldn't wish it on my worst enemy, trying to wake Hunter Thompson up.'

But that didn't stop Thompson playing a gig at The Viper Room, much the same as Johnny's other personal heroes had done in the past; Johnny Cash, Winona's godfather Timothy Leary, and counter-culture luminary Allen Ginsberg, another friend of Winona's father, Michael Horowitz.

'I felt under tremendous pressure,' Johnny would confess later. 'I was so freaked out by the idea of disappointing Hunter. So I did my best to absorb him. My goal was to steal his soul. That's what I wanted to do, to try and take as much of him as possible and put him into my body.'

He elaborates, 'I know it sounds really goofy and all that stuff, but I felt like him, especially when we were doing it. I found it hard to find Johnny in a way because I felt more like Hunter. Even when I was not working, at the weekends, I felt like Hunter.'

But he felt no reservations about accepting the part. Afterwards, he raved how the whole thing from beginning to end had been simply exhilarating. So much so that he was still enamoured with Thompson for months after completing the filming, when he was preparing to join the set of his next movie.

But, then again, he wasn't quite so sure about that. 'Maybe I spent too much time with him. Maybe it had gone too deep. I don't know. It was strange. Hunter's an incredible animal, he's really something to watch. On the one hand, he's this great Southern gentlemen, very sensitive, very caring. But on the other he's very sharp and very cutting. He's a great observer. I mean, the fact that Hunter is still around is a miracle. The way he has lived, the life he has built is like no one else I have ever known.'

It probably didn't help that during filming Johnny was calling Thompson up every day, talking with him for four hours at a time. Gilliam, on the other hand, recalls, 'I had as little to do with Hunter as possible. He has this incredible energy and intelligence. But he also makes you crazy. I was like, "Stay away!" I wanted to get it right, but I did not want to sit there and be constantly aware of what he may or may not be thinking. I just had to go my own way.'

The most pressing issue, of course, would be whether the film could misinterpret the use of drugs. In the book, Duke and Dr Gonzo use ferocious amounts of every drug known to man as they encounter real and imagined characters on their surreal, hallucinogenic journey to Vegas. Could, asked some critics, *Fear and Loathing* be seen as a glorification of drug use?

'Absolutely not,' Johnny sighed, and didn't believe for

one moment that the movie would do that. 'I mean, when you see this film, and you see what these guys ingest, and then feel, and go through, and then expel from their being, it's not like I watch it and go, "Jesus, what a great idea! Let's get really high and puke," or I'd love to see people wandering around with six hairy tits on their back. I mean, come on, this is like a drug nightmare. What were people expecting — *Peter Pan*? This is *Fear and Loathing*.'

At the other end of the spectrum, of course, those same journalists were itching to ask whether he felt the need to experience personally the effects of several drugs to prepare for the role. 'There are people who don't have to do that, I find acting a little more fun.'

But he also knew exactly what they were getting at. A lot of that he put down to speaking too openly with the press about his past. Sure, 'I have dabbled a bit in my youth,' he reflected years later. 'Experimented in various heinous substances. I know what some of them feel like.'

Unfortunately, he concedes, 'There was a time when I was kind of self-destructive. The brain goes weird on you and I don't know whether it was shock of fame, or just part of growing up. You can't be anonymous any more and you don't get used to that — at least, I don't.'

Maybe as a result of those experiences, continues producer Laila Nabulsi, 'he understood the sensitivity of Hunter that a lot of people can't or don't want to see. The basic image of Hunter, all of the craziness and madness and macho stuff, is just part of the story. Hunter is also a very sensitive, deep, thoughtful person, and Johnny has all those qualities. He has those same eyes, that same deep soul.'

Still, it must have been strange for Johnny to play

someone who, in another lifetime, or at least another movie, could easily have turned out to be himself. It had, he explains, 'been screaming to be made into a film since it was published 27 years ago. The book came out of the beginning of the death of the American dream. But Hunter was still out there searching for it, searching madly, hoping that the dream still existed, and all he found was madness in every direction, and tragedy and greed. This book represented a great quest for Hunter, and a kind of exorcism at the same time. It is about hope, it's about insanity, it's about trying to find something out there to believe in.'

One can only imagine what Johnny's parents thought as they watched Johnny playing Raoul Duke, chasing the same dream that they themselves had chased.

Johnny says, 'I think it's a great story that will make people laugh, that will make people think, that will also scare and appal. Some people will see Duke and Dr Gonzo as just a couple of nutcases filling their bodies with heinous chemicals. But it's not about recreation. It's about need.'

All the same, there was an immediate connection between Johnny and Hunter. 'I remember laughing constantly,' recalls Johnny. 'He zeros in on faults and good points immediately. I was with Kate, and I think he went straight for the romantic jugular shit like whether I beat her enough. I probably told him jokingly, "Yeah, she gets a severe beating."'

Johnny also read 'pretty much everything of Hunter's writing that's been published and also lots of stuff that hasn't. I think one of the things that helped with the initial meeting between us was that we're both from Kentucky. Hunter is, beneath it all, a real Southern gentleman.'

The greatest challenge for Johnny, however, was to bond not only emotionally but also physically with his character. 'I tried to make myself look as much like him as possible,' he said. 'I shaved my head on top and just left a kind of short-haired chinchilla around the sides. Hunter's ears are larger than mine, so I wore small devices to make mine poke out a little more. And there's a unique body language that Hunter has, and I could feel myself clicking into that once we started.'

In fact, it was the body language that allowed Johnny to hook into the physical likeness much more easily. His constant bobbing and weaving motion, for instance, and his ever-present cigarette holder functioning almost like an antenna was comparable, some say, to a graceful, if highly offbeat, dancer who is constantly in danger of falling off the stage. Johnny captured that perfectly.

Yet it could have turned out very differently. 'Having Hunter on set for the first time was very intimidating,' explained Johnny. As much, in fact, as it was when Ed Wood's real-life wife visited him on the set during the making of that movie. It was scary, continued Johnny, because 'I was afraid that it might be upsetting for him. But he was great.' Not only that, but he was also very supportive throughout the entire project. 'To allow me to, in a way, become his shadow, in his home, and on the road, 24 hours a day, for months. I was very blessed to have that.

'I really did become him in this film; in fact, too much. He is all the things I want to be — sensitive, cutting, sharp, observant. When I lived with him I wanted to swallow his thoughts and emotions. Actor Bill Murray (who played Thompson in 1980's *Where the Buffalo Roam*) called me up before we started filming and said, "This is your warning call. Hunter never leaves you. It will take years to shake him off." And he was right.'

Fear and Loathing in Las Vegas was scheduled for a May 1998 release in the States, and for September in Britain following its première at the Cannes Film Festival. It was among the competition entries judged by Martin Scorsese's jury, that interestingly enough included Winona Ryder.

The critical reaction was muted, if a little bemused. The movie, like the book, lacked plot, the general consensus ran, even if praise for Johnny's performance far exceeded the expectations of the film itself.

There was, however, a sting in the tail. Johnny's performance, no matter how good or bad it was, was seen by many as 'another of his quirky roles in a career that has studiously avoided the mainstream'.

But why, asked those same critics, does he avoid the mainstream? 'It could be ignorance,' Johnny attempted to explain. But then again, 'It could be that I'm just incredibly thick and dumb. But it takes commitment. I feel deeply committed to these characters I've chosen because I have an interest in them. I find them stimulating and I think it's something I can do that's maybe a little different. I think it's very easy to take the paved road, and I think it's very boring.'

He even blamed that commitment to his break-up with Kate Moss. Their on-off-on romance now seemed off for good, and Johnny knew exactly where the blame should lie. 'I let my career get in the way and I didn't give her the attention I should have done. We had so much going for us, but I've just been very stupid. I was a horrific pain in the butt to live with. Trust me, I'm a total moron at times.

'We ended up living apart and only talking on the phone every two weeks. I really feel like I blew it with Kate. There's a big part of me that really misses her and I keep wondering why we aren't together, thinking about starting a family.'

But maybe that was another reason why his relationship with Kate didn't really work out, as much as it hadn't worked out with Winona. Both had burgeoning careers in their respective fields, and perhaps children did not rank quite so highly in their personal ambitions as they did in Johnny's.

All the same, that didn't stop Kate joining him at Cannes, or at the Las Vegas première. It even sparked new speculation of a reconciliation. It probably didn't help that Johnny was still wearing the huge silver skull ring she once gave him. They were, after all, nothing more than just good friends, Johnny insisted. 'She was in town and she was going to be seeing the movie anyway. Everyone's thinking, "Oh my God, they're back together." But we're not.'

Three months before Cannes, Johnny and Kate's appearance at the 1998 Rolling Stones Madison Square Garden gig with Ethan Hawke and Uma Thurman did much the same. 'Johnny Depp and Kate Moss appear to be back together,' shouted the *New York Daily News*. On leaving the concert, the paper continued, 'Depp was in high spirits. When *paparrazzo* John Barrett dropped his house keys, Depp picked them up, then asked Barrett to "prove" they belonged to him. Barrett did, prompting Depp to toss them back on the sidewalk.'

Johnny's next role appeared just as he was wrapping

up work on *Fear and Loathing in Las Vegas*. His agent, Tracy Jacobs, probably thought it was perfect for him. Or at least, that it would make a welcome change.

Rand Ravitch's *The Astronaut's Wife*, still only tentatively titled, would commence filming on 14 January 1998 for release late the following year. Even in pre-production it sounded promising.

Imagine it, 'Johnny Depp hunted by aliens,' warned one of many journalists visiting the location filming in New York. 'Shades, black coat, cigarillo in his mouth, hair short as never before, this is the cool look in which Depp is hurrying through the streets of New York. At the top of a subway staircase he stops quickly and grabs a black attaché case which a young woman has put on the railing only seconds before. Carrying the explosive documents under his arm he disappears in the crowd.'

It was, according to production company New Line's advance information, a spine chilling, psychological thriller about a woman driven to the brink of madness by the terrifying suspicion that the father of her unborn twins is not the man she married — he may not even be human.

Jillian and Spencer Armacost, played by Charlize Theron and Johnny, are the perfect couple, living the American dream, until one fateful day when Spencer, an astronaut on a routine Shuttle mission, mysteriously loses contact for two minutes with mission control. What happened in those eerie two minutes of silence Jillian will never know.

Although Spencer returns home alive and is decorated by the President as a hero, Jillian begins to realise that she is witness to a terrifying metamorphosis.

When Spencer announces that he is quitting the space programme for a job as a defence contractor in New York, a city that he has always hated, Jillian reluctantly agrees to his decision.

Once settled in New York, Jillian and Spencer resume a normal life — on the surface. When Jillian discovers she is pregnant with twins, Spencer is thrilled. Yet the happy news is overshadowed by haunting visions of outer space and strange sounds that creep into Jillian's dreams. She is confused and scared — her dreams seem like reality and her life with Spencer has dissolved into strange days of loneliness and confusion.

Her fears and suspicions increase when Sherman Reese, a NASA official who was fired for 'paranoid delusions' about the incident in space, tracks her down and shares his findings that something did indeed occur during those missing two minutes, something horrifying that has changed Spencer and made him an unwilling participant in an other-worldly attempt to invade earth.

With Spencer becoming increasingly deranged and his actions and whereabouts a complete mystery, Jillian knows she is in a race against time to find the truth about her husband before he changes the future of mankind for ever.

With his work on *The Astronaut's Wife* completed, maybe Johnny should have taken a break. But he had already committed himself to another movie, and he was damned if he was going to pull out.

Empire magazine, in its countdown to future films, would suggest that for *The Ninth Gate*, 'Depp remains in similar territory as the upcoming *Astronaut's Wife* for this follow-up. Cutting back on his usual fee for the chance to work with Roman Polanski, the film, based on the 1997 novel *The Club Dumas* by Arturo Perez-Reverte will see Depp as a rare books expert who, while attempting to track down two copies of an ancient demonic text, becomes embroiled in a supernatural conspiracy over which he has no control. Add the Polanski trademarks of a multi-million dollar cast, including Frank Langella, Emmanuelle Seigner and Lena Nolin, and some picturesque continental settings for the unexplained events, the outlook is decidedly rosy — especially for those who prefer their horror on the intelligent side.'

It was here, during location filming in Paris, that Johnny would first clap eyes on Vanessa Paradis without even knowing who she was. Twelve years earlier, Vanessa's first single, 'Joe Le Taxi', had stormed the international charts when she was just 14 years old.

By then she was about to make her mark on French cinema with her début in 1989's *Noce Blanch*, and over the next ten years would feature in another four features with the much acclaimed *The Girl on the Bridge* in 1998. With her Lolita-esque looks she also made her mark in the world of fashion and photography as the new face for Chanel's Coco perfume and the body for Jean-Paul Goude's pictures.

But when Johnny spotted her at the bar of the Hotel Costes, he knew little about her. But that didn't stop him buying her a drink, and in an echo of his meeting Kate Moss, invited her over to his table. Even if he wasn't quite ready to dive into a new relationship, he certainly underestimated the strength of his own emotions.

Only a few months after they met, they were sharing

a flat in the upstate Montmartre district of Paris, and a few months after that she was pregnant with his child. And if everything went according to plan, Johnny and Vanessa's daughter, Lily-Rose Melody Depp, would be born on 27 May 1999, in Paris, France. She was.

'I want to carry a child, to conceive it and to feed it,' she had said in an interview the previous year. Johnny, too, had said much the same at Cannes just over a year earlier. 'There's a part of me that would love to settle down and have a couple of kids, a wife and goldfish and watch television every night till eleven. I want to be an old man with a beer belly sitting on a porch. A part of me would love that, but another part of me needs to roll round in the mud.'

Even Vanessa's parents were delighted. 'She has introduced Johnny to the whole family and they find him charming,' revealed one of their friends. 'He obviously dotes on her.' But according to some, the news would be more than heartbreaking to Kate Moss, who at the time was recovering from exhaustion at London's Priory clinic, where patients are treated for depression, eating disorders, and drug and alcohol abuse.

It was from where Kate, shortly before her discharge, would almost burn the place down, just as Winona had almost done five years earlier in her Portugal hotel room, when she fell asleep with a burning cigarette between her fingers.

But according to Jess Hallett of Kate's agency, Storm Models, 'The fire was out before the three fire engines arrived. It was all over very quickly and it was no big deal. Kate certainly wasn't embarrassed by it. More than anything else, she thought it was amusing.'

That is probably true. At the same time, though, the press couldn't help writing about how the incident had seemingly been sparked off by Johnny himself. He apparently decided to cheer Kate up with a 'get well soon' BMW. She was so excited, noted New York's *Daily Post*, 'that she asked the chauffeur to take her for a spin around the grounds'. He did. The trouble was, Kate had placed one of her meditating candles too close to the scarf her mother had given her, and it went up in flames. So did her room. It was, observed London's *Evening Standard*, the second of 'Depp's ex-girlfriends to accidentally start a fire on breaking up with the actor'.

It would even invite rumours that the couple were back together. According to Dominic Mohan writing in the *Sun* less than a month later, 'They spent an intimate evening together at a private party in Notting Hill, West London, where my sources tell me they were nattering for hours. And although they left separately, Johnny's car and driver were spotted minutes later outside Kate's nearby home despite Johnny's impending fatherhood with Vanessa Paradis.'

Johnny, of course, let the speculation drift over his head, but still the stories of a reconciliation rattled on. Another in America's *National Enquirer* went even further when it suggested, 'There's no doubt about it, Johnny's still in love with Kate and she with him.' According to one insider talking to the same tabloid, 'When Vanessa read British news reports about Johnny and Kate getting back together she was hopping mad.'

It was the same when Johnny and Winona were together. Rumours abounded that both had been stepping out with other young stars. Now, as then, Johnny, Kate and Vanessa ignored the tattle, refusing even to dignify the tales with a response.

Whatever else, Johnny, now barely 36, still had kids on his mind. 'I thought the time was right. I'm getting broody. What scares me is the thought of not having kids some day. I'm ready to have a young 'un. But I also have a traditional idea of marriage, too — a home in the country, a picket fence, a couple of dogs. It's a big dream of mine.'

Less than a month after he had fininshed *The Ninth Gate*, Johnny boarded a plane for London. Tim Burton, his old ally from *Edward Scissorhands* and *Ed Wood*, would be waiting for him when he got there, and having worked with Johnny twice before, he knew exactly what he would be getting — one of America's most respected actors.

Once again, it was no surprise that Johnny agreed to join forces with Burton, this time for Andrew Kevin Walker's adaptation of Washington Irving's classic story, *The Legend of Sleepy Hollow*.

With its original unwieldy title changed to the snappier *Sleepy Hollow*, the movie would, according to *Entertainment Weekly*, be a huge departure from the original tale. In many ways, it picks up where the classic left off, and there would be far more focus on blood and guts.

Similarly, the film's setting, according to one observer, depicts the unexpected strangeness that is strangely expected from a Burton movie. 'Imagine the old scary forest you used to hang out in as a kid. Imagine digging this whole forest up — trees, hills and all — and planting it in the middle of a studio. Well, that's sort of what it was like. But better. You see, while I was convinced that it was real, there was something unreal about it.

'You know the opening of *Beetlejuice* — the way there is something unsettling about the landscape? Well, that's just what they got here. The trees were devoid of leaves, and were painted to look quite ghostly. The backdrops were all quite impressionistic, and mainly monochrome. The more you looked at this forest, the more unsettling it became.'

And that was the opinion of the clutch of young actors recruited for the other parts. Johnny had already agreed to appear as Ichabod Crane long before the rest of the cast was assembled. The decision to cast Christina Ricci, Johnny's co-star from *Fear and Loathing*, as Katrina Van Tassel, was equally instinctive. She remembers her first meeting with Johnny on the set of *Mermaids* very well, mainly because he was with Winona at the time.

'I was nine years old and didn't know what "gay" was, and when I asked Winona, she said, "I can't tell you, ask Johnny." Johnny explained how there were different theories about why people were gay, what it was to be gay, and — this is what I couldn't figure out — how gay people have sex. He was amazing like that. Eight years later, I'm going into rehearsal on *Fear and Loathing* and he remembered me, our discussions, and my mother, Sarah. He said to her, "Hi, Sarah, how are you?" and asked about my brothers. He was really sweet, kind and gentle.'

Even as he worked on the Tim Burton movie, and awaited the release of his 1998 cameo as himself in the French arthouse movie *LA without a Map*, Johnny was being tentatively linked opposite his old flame Winona Ryder in Michaelangelo Antonioni's latest film *Just To Be*

Together. Johnny's publicist, however, had not even heard of it. Nor had Winona's. But according to *Now* magazine, Matt Damon, Winona's current boyfriend, was more concerned than most.

He adores Winona, confided one of those convenient 'friends' who always seem to be on hand to comment about showbiz affairs of the heart. 'Johnny has always protested that he still loves Winona, while she has always held a special place for him in her heart because he was her first real love.'

Such a premise was not altogether to anyone's benefit, least of all the tabloids. 'It's not as if Johnny and I are buddy-buddy,' affirmed Winona. 'But it's nice to know we can have a friendship. It's good to be able to think about him without having a horrible feeling in the pit of my stomach, or cringing or feeling heartbroken or like he hates me. After you break up, you go through all those feelings.'

But break-ups, Winona elaborates, are 'hard for anybody, but it's particularly tough when your life is being documented and you see the person's picture everywhere. Most people don't have that added problem when they break up. Our break-up was like the never-ending story because it was such a public thing. We didn't know how to break up. I had my first real relationship with Johnny. It was a fiercely deep love that I don't know that I'll ever .... The first love is like that, isn't it? It was a wild time back then.'

Not so wild was the fact that Winona had asked Johnny to appear in a cameo role she thought he might like in the live-action version of the *Scooby Doo* cartoon she was developing with Denise Di Novi, Johnny and Winona's old ally from *Edward Scissorhands*. Johnny accepted and would commence filming late in 1999 for a Christmas release the following year.

But, of course, both stars had been linked to projects before that had never come to anything. One of those projects that had been doing the Hollywood rounds ever since the couple had made *Edward Scissorhands* together was a film version of *Dream Lovers*, the true story of Bobby Darin and Sandra Dee, based on the book by Barry Levinson, Darin's son, and at the time, linked Johnny alongside Winona in the title roles.

According to the Internet, eight years later, Johnny was still in the running for the part. And interestingly enough, Winona had been reading the book when she was shooting *Boys* two years earlier.

And another biopic, *Empire: The Life, Legend and Madness of Howard Hughes*, also linked Johnny to the title role for what many believed would be his most challenging part.

A millionaire since 18 years of age, Hughes was a celebrity playboy made famous by producing such films as *Hell's Angels* and *The Outlaw*. Above all, he was made famous for his love of flying. His romances with some of Hollywood's most beautiful women were equally notorious, Jean Harlow and Katharine Hepburn among them. More tragically, of course, he was best known for his descent into isolation. It began after he survived a near-fatal air crash and became dependent on prescription drugs, much the same as Elvis Presley would decades later.

At the time of his death, he was long-haired, long-fingernailed and confined to his bedroom for much of the time. Not only that, but he had developed a debilitating fear of infection and disease. According to the book, on which the film would be based, his arms were spotted with broken ends of hypodermic needles embedded in his skin.

There was even talk of Johnny linking up again with Terry Gilliam, his director from *Fear and Loathing in Las Vegas*, for a film version of Miguel de Cervantes' classic, *Don Quixote*. Another project being slated for production also linked Johnny to *The White Hotel*, D M Thomas's novel, which, if the rumours were true, would reunite him with his old ally from *Arizona Dream*, Emir Kusturica. Nicole Kidman, Juliette Binoche, Holly Hunter, and Jennifer Jason Leigh were all being sought for the lead role opposite him.

At the same time, Roman Polanski, Johnny's director from *The Ninth Gate* presented him with the César, the French equivalent of the Oscar that honoured his contribution to the arts. Johnny responded with sheer delight and a taped message he prepared because his French, he openly admitted, wasn't that great.

'I don't really understand the concept of praise in general and I hate the idea of competition. The only person against whom I'm fighting is me, to go as far as possible each time in my work. Nobody is better, we are just all different. But it's a great honour to receive this present from France because I love and respect your country which gives the chance to art to stay alive. To everyone who followed me on this road, I'm deeply grateful. Thanks very much.'

Enjoying the freedom of weekends away from filming, Johnny and Vanessa continued spending time together, unaware of what was about to hit them that February 1999 evening when they left London's Mirabelle restuarant.

Neither, for that matter, did the photographers waiting outside to snap their pictures.

'We had been tipped off that Depp was at the restaurant and when we arrived, he was already there,' explained one of the photographers. 'He came to one of the side doors and wanted one of the cameras, and kept saying he didn't want his picture taken. He said if we took a picture he'd smash our heads in. He'd kill us. We just thought he was being over-dramatic. Shortly afterwards, his girlfriend came out covered up and one of the photographers took a couple of pictures.'

That was it, continued the photographer, 'Depp said, "Do you want a fucking mess? I'll fucking kill you." Then he came out with a piece of wood in his hand. He must have picked it up inside. He threatened to smash our heads in and muscled up to each of us and chased us, threatening us with this piece of wood. He chased us down the road. All the time, none of us took a single picture.

'We called the police after this had gone on for five minutes. Then the guy with him came up and pushed my camera into my face, cutting my head. I had started to walk back towards the restaurant as the flashing lights appeared. Depp chased me again with the wood tucked under his arm, and became very nasty. Within seconds, the police jumped out and grabbed him. He still had the wood in his possession. Even as he was being shoved into the back of a police van, he kept lashing out until the police grabbed the wood from him.'

Whatever the reasons for Johnny's outburst, and they were probably to do with his rebuttal of media exposure, Johnny would not make any comments about the incident afterwards. That was left to his spokesperson and Scotland Yard. 'A 35-year-old man was cautioned and released without charge. He is not on bail and does not have to report back to us.'

Unfortunately, there were a lot of people who roundly criticised Johnny's behaviour. Not even the headlines of HOLLYWOOD WILDMAN'S NIGHT OF SHAME could help his defence. More fatefully, of course, were the pictures of his arrest adorning the tabloids the following morning that did nothing more than add fuel to the fire.

But according to Winona Ryder, 'He's such a nice guy. Certainly some of the things I hear about him I know aren't true, you know, some of the rumours. All the bad boy stuff. He's not a bad boy, he's a good boy, and he never causes any real damage. He's a really wonderful guy.'

As Johnny celebrates his first decade in the entertainment industry, he has finally established himself among the select few stars who could celebrate a decade of top-line successes. Even when his movies were bad, his own reviews were great, and even when his movies were lacklustre, he himself sparkled. And when that sparkle began losing its allure, he knew enough to re-invent it, and to do so with the minimum of fuss.

Although he would join Dawn French for a Comic Relief sketch from *The Vicar of Dibley*, he still maintained a comparatively low profile, further evidence that this intensely private person is also intensely modest.

After the years of uncertainty and public scrutiny that marred much of his career, and the awful trial of trying to live down his 'bad boy' image while retaining his own personality, Johnny is now in the enviable position of not having to care how other people see him. As long as he is happy with his own performance, that is all that matters.

It is a remarkably mature attitude to find in one whose decisions and general refusal to compromise his goals and beliefs to please others might have ruined a lesser talent and would certainly have crippled a less resolute one, all the more so since Johnny works in a field that actively discourages such individuality.

In an industry that has spent nearly a century churning out stereotypes, Johnny Depp has made a virtue of individuality, of retaining his spirit, and of remaining himself. And in doing so, he has created a body of work that stands proud in its integrity.

And that may be the key to his success. Although Johnny makes his living in Hollywood, he doesn't have to live there as well.

Filmography

A Nightmare on Elm Street (1984)
USA 1984, 91 minutes. Directed by Wes Craven. Screenplay by Wes Craven. Production Company: New Line Cinema/Media Home Entertainment/Smart Egg Picture for The Elm Street Venture. Cast: John Saxon (Lieutenant Thompson), Ronee Blakely (Marge Thompson), Heather Langenkamp (Nancy Thompson), Amada Wyss (Tina Gray), Nick Corri (Rod Lane), *Johnny Depp (Glen Lantz)*, Robert Englund (Freddy Krueger).

Private Resort (1985)
USA 1985, 79 minutes. Directed by George Bowers. Screenplay by Gordon Mitchell. Story by Ken Segull and Alann Wenkus and Gordon Mitchell. Production Company: Tristar Pictures. Cast: Rob Morrow (Ben), *Johnny Depp (Jack)*, Emily Longstreth (Patti), Karyn O'Bryan (Dana),

Hector Elizondon (The Maestro), Dody Goodman (Mrs Rawlings), Tony Azito (Reeves), Hilary Shapiro (Shirley), Leslie Easterbrook (Bobby Sue), Michael Bowen (Scott), Lisa London (Alice), Andrew Clay (Curt), Ron House (The Barber), Greg Wynne (Mike).

Slow Burn (TV, 1986)

USA 1986, 94 minutes. Directed by Matthew Chapman. Screenplay by Matthew Chapman. Production Company: Castle Burning Productions in association with MCA Pay TV Programming Inc. Cast: Eric Roberts (Jacob Asch), Beverly D'Angelo (Laine Fleischer), Dennis Lipscomb (Ron McDonald), Raymond J Barry (Gerald McMurty), Ann Shedeen (Mona), Emily Longstreth (Pam Draper), *Johnny Depp (Donnie Fleischer)*, Henry Gibson (Robert), Dan Hedaya (Simon Fleischer).

Platoon (1986)

USA 1986, 120 minutes. Directed by Oliver Stone. Screenplay by Oliver Stone. Production Company: Hemdale Film Corporation. Cast: Tom Berenger (Sergeant Barnes), Willem Dafoe (Sergeant Elias), Charlie Sheen (Chris Taylor), Forest Whitaker (Big Harold), Francesco Quinn (Rhah), John C McGinley (Sergeant O'Neill), Richard Edson (Sal), Kevin Dillon (Bunny), Reggie Johnson (Junior), Keith David (King), *Johnny Depp (Lerner)*.

21 Jump Street (TV, 4th series, 1987–1990)
Pilot: *21 Jump Street* USA 1987, 120 minutes. Directed by Kim Manners. Screenplay by Patrick Hasburgh. Series created by Patrick Hasburgh & Stephen J Cannell. Production Company: Stephen J Cannell Productions Inc. Cast: *Johnny Depp (Tom Hanson)*, Frederic Forrest (Captain Jenko), Holly Robinson (Judy Hoffs), Peter DeLuise (Doug Penhall), Dustin Nguyen (H T Ioki).

Series: *21 Jump Street*, 1987–1991, 50-minute episodes, 103 episodes, 5 seasons. Regular cast: *Johnny Depp (Officer Tom Hanson)* [Seasons 1–4], Holly Robinson (Detective Judy Hoffs), Peter DeLuise (Officer Doug Penhall), Dustin Nguyen (Officer Vinh Van Tran, aka Harry Truman Ioki).

Cry Baby (1990)
USA 1990, 85 minutes. Directed by John Waters. Screenplay by John Waters. Production Company: Imagine Entertainment. Cast: *Johnny Depp (Wade 'Cry Baby' Walker)*, Amy Locane (Allison), Susan Tyrell (Ramona), Polly Bergen (Mrs Vernon-Williams), Iggy Pop (Belverdere), Ricki Lake (Pepper), Traci Lords (Wanda), Troy Donahue (Hatchet's Father), Mink Stole (Hatchet's Mother), Joe Dallesandro (Milton's Father), Patricia Hearst (Wanda's Mother), Willem Dafoe (Hateful Guard).

Edward Scissorhands (1990)

USA 1990, 90 minutes. Directed by Tim Burton. Screenplay by Caroline Thompson, based on a story by Tim Burton and Caroline Thompson. Production Company: Twentieth Century Fox. Cast: *Johnny Depp (Edward Scissorhands)*, Winona Ryder (Kim Boggs), Dianne Wiest (Peg Boggs), Anthony Michael Hall (Jim), Kathy Baker (Joyce Monroe), Robert Oliveri (Kevin Boggs), Vincent Price (The Inventor), Alan Arkin (Bill Boggs).

Freddy's Dead: The Final Nightmare (1991, Cameo)

USA 1991, 89 minutes. 3D Sequence. Directed by Rachael Talalay. Screenplay by Michael DeLuca, based on a story by Rachael Talalay. Production Company: New Line Cinema. Cast: Robert Englund (Freddy Krueger), Lisa Zane (Maggie Burroughs), Shon Greenblatt (John), Yaphet Kotto (Doc), Tom Arnold (Childless Man), Mrs Tom Arnold aka Roseanne Barr (Childless Woman), *Oprah Noodlemantra [aka Johnny Depp] (Teenager on TV)*, Tobe Sexton (Teen Freddy).

Arizona Dream (1991)

USA/France 1991, 141 minutes. Directed by Emir Kusturica. Screenplay by David Atkins, based on a story by David Atkins and Emir Kusturica. Production Company: Constellation/UGC/Hachette Première. With the participation of Ministère de la Culture et de la Communication (Centre

National de la Cinematographie). Cast: *Johnny Depp (Axel Blakmar)*, Jerry Lewis (Leo Sweetie), Faye Dunaway (Elaine), Lili Taylor (Grace), Vincent Gallo (Paul Blakmar), Michael J Pollard (Fabian), Sal Jenco (Man at Phone), Iggy Pop (Man with Pumpkin).

Benny and Joon (1993)

USA 1993, 99 minutes. Directed by Jeremiah Chechik. Screenplay by Barry Berman, based on a story by Barry Berman and Leslie McNeil. Production Company: MGM. Cast: *Johnny Depp (Sam)*, Mary Stuart Masterson (Joon Pearl), Aidan Quinn (Benny Pearl), Julianne Moore (Ruthie), Oliver Platt (Eric), CCH Pounder (Dr Garvey), Dan Hedaya (Thomas), William H Macy (Randy Burch), Noon Orsatti, Dan Kamin (Patrons).

What's Eating Gilbert Grape? (1993)

USA 1993, 118 minutes. Directed by Lasse Hallstrom. Screenplay by Peter Hedges, based on his novel. Production Company: Paramount. Cast: *Johnny Depp (Gilbert Grape)*, Juliette Lewis (Becky), Mary Steenburgen (Betty Carver), Leonardo DiCaprio (Arnie Grape), John C Reilly (Tucker Van Dyke), Darlene Cates (Bonnie Grape), Laura Harrington (Amy Grape), Mary Kate Schellhardt (Ellen Grape), Crispin Glover (Bobby McBurney), Kevin Tighe (Mr Carver), Robert Hedges (Minister).

Ed Wood (1994)

USA 1994, 127 minutes. Black and white. Directed by Tim Burton. Screenplay by Scott Alexander and Larry Karaszewski, based on the book *Nightmare of Ecstasy* by Rudolph Grey. Production Company: Buena Vista. Cast: *Johnny Depp (Ed Wood)*, Martin Landau (Bela Lugosi), Sarah Jessica Parker (Dolores Fuller), Patricia Arquette (Kathy O'Hara), Jeffrey Jones (Criswell), G D Spradin (Reverend Lemon), Vincent D'Onofrio (Orson Welles), Bill Murray (Bunny Breckinridge), Lisa Marie (Vampira), George 'The Animal' Steele (Tor Johnson), Juliet Landau (Loretta King), Conrad Brooks (Bartender), Gregory Walcott (Potential Backer).

Don Juan DeMarco (1994)

USA 1994, 97 minutes. Directed by Jeremy Leven. Screenplay by Jeremy Leven. Production Company: New Line Productions for American Zoetrope. Cast: *Johnny Depp (Don Juan DeMarco)*, Marlon Brando (Jack Mickler), Faye Dunaway (Marilyn Mickler), Bob Dishy (Dr Paul Showalter), Geraldine Pailhas (Dona Ana), Talisa Soto (Dona Julia), Rachel Ticotin (Dona Inez), Marita Geraghty (Woman in Restaurant), Richard Sarafian (Detective Sy Tobias), Tresa Hughes (Grandmother DeMarco), Jo Champa (Sultana Gulbeyaz).

Dead Man (1995)

USA 1995, 134 minutes. Black and white. Directed by Jim Jarmusch. Screenplay by Jim Jarmusch. Production Company: A12 Gauge Production with Pandora Film, JVC, Newmarket Capital Group and LP. Cast: *Johnny Depp (William Blake)*, Crispin Glover (The Fireman), John Hurt (John Scholfield), John North (Mr Olafsen), Robert Mitchum (John Dickson), Gibby Haynes (Man in the Alley), Mili Avital (Thel Russell), Peter Schrum (Drunk), Gabriel Byrne (Charlie Dickson), Lance Henriksen (Cole Wilson), Gary Farmer (Nobody), Iggy Pop (Salvatore 'Sally' Jenko), Alfred Molina (Trading Post Missionary).

Nick of Time (1995)

USA 1995, 95 minutes. Directed by John Badham. Screenplay by Patrick Sheane and Ebbe Roe Smith. Production Company: Paramount Pictures. Cast: *Johnny Depp (Gene Watson)*, Christopher Walken (Mr Smith), Roma Maffia (Ms Jones), Charles Dutton (Huey), Marsha Mason (Eleanor Grant), Gloria Reuben (Krista Brooks), Courtney Chase (Lynn Wason), Bill Smitrovich (Mr White), G D Spradlin (Mystery Man).

Divine Rapture (1995, uncompleted)

USA 1995, 20 minutes of footage shot. Directed by Thom Eberhardt. Screenplay by Thom Eberhardt. Production Company: Cinefin. Cast: *Johnny Depp*, Marlon Brando, Debra Winger, John Hurt.

The Brave (1996)

USA 1996. *Directed by Johnny Depp. Screenplay by Johnny Depp*, Paul McCudden and D P Depp. Production Company: Acappella Pictures. Cast: *Johnny Depp (Raphael)*, Marlon Brando (McCarthy), Marshall Bell (Larry), Elpidia Carrillo (Rita), Frederic Forrest (Lou Sr), Clarence Williams III (Father Stratton), Max Perlich (Lou Jr), Luis Guzman (Luis), Cody Lightning (Frankie), Nicole Mancera (Marta), Floyd 'Red Crow' Westerman (Papa).

Donnie Brasco (1996)

USA 1996. Directed by Mike Newell. Screenplay by Paul Attanasio, based on *The Book* by Joseph D Pistone. Production Company: Tristar Pictures. Cast: *Johnny Depp (Donnie)*, Al Pacino (Lefty), Michael Madsen (Sonny), Bruno Kirby (Nicky), James Russo (Paulie), Anne Heche (Maggie), Zeljko Ivanek (Tim Curley), Gerry Becker (Dean Blandford), Robert Miano (Sonny Red), Brian Taratina (Bruno).

LA Without A Map (1998)

1998. Directed by Mika Kaurismaki. Screenplay by Richard Rayner and Mika Kaurismaki based on the novel *Los Angeles Without a Map* by Richard Rayner. Production Company: Dan Films–Euro American Films–Marianna Films. Cast: David Tennant (Richard), Vinessa Shaw (Barbara), Julie Delpy (Julie), Vincent Gallo (Moss), Cameron Bancroft (Patterson), James Le Gros (Takowsky), Saskia Reeves (Joy),

Steve Huison (Billy), Lisa Edelstein (Sandra), Joe Dallesandro (Michael), Jerzy Skolimowsky (Minister), Amanda Plummer (Pool Owner), Anouk Aimee, Robert Davi, *Johnny Depp*, Montel Hellman (Themselves).

Fear and Loathing in Las Vegas (1998)
USA 1998. Directed by Terry Gilliam. Screenplay by Alex Cox and Tod Davies, based on the book *Fear and Loathing in Las Vegas* by Hunter S Thompson. Production Company: Rhino Films. Cast: *Johnny Depp (Raoul Duke)*, Benicio Del Toro (Oscar Acosta), Gary Busby (Highway Patrolman), Toby Maguire (Hitch-Hiker), Christina Ricci (Lucy), Harry Dean Stanton (Judge), Cameron Diaz (Blonde TV Reporter), Lyle Lovett (Road Person), Ellen Barkin (North Star Waitress).

The Astronaut's Wife (1999)
USA 1999. Directed by Rand Ravich. Screenplay by Rand Ravich. Cast: Blair Brown (Shelley McLaren), Nick Cassavetes (Alex Streck), *Johnny Depp (Spencer Armacost)*, Clea Du Vall (Nan), Joe Morton (Sherman Reese), Donna Murphy (Natalie Streck), Tom Noonan (Jackson McLaren), Charlize Theron (Jillian Armacost).

The Ninth Gate (1999)
USA 1999. Directed by Roman Polanski. Screenplay by John Brownjohn and Roman Polanski. Cast: Frank Langella, *Johnny Depp*, Lena Olin, James Russo, Emmanuelle Seigner.

Sleepy Hollow (1999)

USA 1999. Directed by Tim Burton. Screenplay by Andrew Kevin Walker based on the book by Washington Irving. Production Company: Paramount. Cast: *Johnny Depp (Ichabod Crane)*, Christina Ricci (Katrina Van Tassel), Casper Van Dien (Brom Van Brunt), Michael Gambon (Baltus Van Tassel), Lisa Marie (Lady Van Tassel), Miranda Richardson (Old Crone), Jeffrey Jones (Steenwyck).